READY TO WRITE MORE

From Paragraph To Essay

SECOND EDITION

Karen Blanchard

Christine Root

LONGMAN ON THE **WEB**

Longman.com offers online resources for teachers and students. Access our Companion Websites, our online catalog, and our local offices around the world.

Visit us at **longman.com**.

Longman

Ready to Write More: From Paragraph to Essay
Second Edition

Pearson Education, 10 Bank Street, White Plains, NY 10606

Senior acquisitions editor: Laura Le Dréan
Senior development editor: Paula H. Van Ells
Vice president, director of design and production: Rhea Banker
Director of electronic production: Aliza Greenblatt
Executive managing editor: Linda Moser
Production manager: Ray Keating
Production editor: Andréa C. Basora
Director of manufacturing: Patrice Fraccio
Senior manufacturing buyer: Dave Dickey
Photo research and text permissions: Dana Klinek
Cover and text design: Pat Wosczyk
Cover image: Marjory Dressler Photo-Graphics
Text composition: Rainbow Graphics
Text art: Daisy de Puthod pp. 81–82, 111, 130; Jessica Miller p. 79; Jim Russell pp. 15, 42, 121, 160, 161; Jill Wood pp. 22, 89, 99, 101, 107, 167
Illustrations and photographs: p. 3, reprinted by permission: Tribune Media Services; p. 33, courtesy of David Root; p. 51, reprinted by permission: Tribune Media Services; p. 58, courtesy of New York State Department of Economic Development; p. 61, © AP/Wide World Photos; p. 64, © Andy Crawford/Dorling Kindersley Media Library; p. 70, © Andrew D. Bernstein, courtesy of the NBA; p. 84, © 1996, reprinted courtesy of Bunny Hoest and *Parade* magazine; p. 93, courtesy of the U.S. Department of Agriculture and the U.S. Department of Health and Human Services; p. 104 top, © Jonathan Nourok/PhotoEdit; p. 104 bottom, © Tom Carter/PhotoEdit; p. 105 top, © AP/Wide World Photos; p. 105 center, © Mark Stephenson/CORBIS; p. 105 bottom, © Duomo/CORBIS; p. 146, The Mainichi Newspapers Co., Ltd.; p. 150, © Bettmann/CORBIS; p. 155, Number 10, 1949. Jackson Pollock, American, 1912–1956. Oil, enamel and aluminum paint on canvas mounted on panel. 46.04 x 272.41 cm (18 1/8 x 107 1/4 in.). © 2003 Museum of Fine Arts, Boston. Tompkins Collection and Sophie M. Friedman Fund. 1971.638; p. 156, Watson and the Shark, 1778; John Singleton Copley, American 1738–1815). Oil on canvas; 72 1/4 x 90 3/8 in. (183.5 x 229.6 cm). Gift of Mrs. George von Lengerke Meyer, 89.481. Courtesy, Museum of Fine Arts, Boston. Reproduced with permission. © 2002 Museum of Fine Arts, Boston; p. 157, CHRISTINA' S WORLD 1948, tempera on panel © Andrew Wyeth. The Museum of Modern Art, New York; p. 158 left, © Gail Mooney/CORBIS; p. 158 right, courtesy of Mrs. H. F. Heyden; p. 164, © The New Yorker Collection 1995 J. P. Rini from cartoon bank.com. All Rights Reserved; p. 164, NON SEQUITUR © 1996 Wiley Miller. Dist. BY UNIVERSAL PRESS SYNDICATE. Reprinted with Permission. All rights reserved.

Text credits appear on page 183

Library of Congress Cataloging-in-Publication Data

Blanchard, Karen Lourie, 1951–
    Ready to write more: from paragraph to essay / Karen Blanchard, Christine Root.— 2nd ed.
      p. cm.
    ISBN 0-13-048468-7
    1. English language—Textbooks for foreign speakers. 2. English language—Composition and exercises. I. Root, Christine Baker, 1945– II. Title.

PEl128.B587 2003
808′.042—dc21

2003054506

ISBN 0-13-048468-7

Printed in the United States of America
8 9 10—BAH—09 08 07 06

Acknowledgments

We are grateful to several people whose contributions strengthened this book. Thank you to Kathy Buruca and Robby Steinberg for their inspired suggestions and to Daniel Blanchard, Alan Bronstein, Hasan Halkali, and Matthew Root for allowing us to use their essays. Thanks also to Dan Hogan and David Root, our management and technical consultants, and to Ian Root, apprentice editor extraordinaire. Finally, thanks to Allen Ascher, Laura Le Dréan, and Paula Van Ells at Longman for their steadfast support.

Reviewers

Mary Caldwell, El Paso Community College, El Paso, TX
Ingrid Cardena, El Paso Community College, El Paso, TX
Judith Di Leo, Mount Ida College, Newton, MA
Karen Newbrun Einstein, Santa Rosa Junior College, Santa Rosa, CA
Sheila Goldstein, Rockland Community College, Suffern, NY
Kevin Keane, Osaka Women's University, Kawachinagano, Japan

To the memory of Michael Blanchard:
for his love of good writing and his enduring spirit.

Contents

Quick Reference Guide

Introduction

Ready to Write More, Second Edition, is a writing skills text designed for intermediate and high-intermediate students who are ready to write more than paragraph-level pieces. It is intended to build on the fundamentals of paragraph writing that students learned in *Get Ready to Write* and *Ready to Write* and to give them the confidence they need to venture into the realm of writing longer pieces.

APPROACH

Ready to Write More is based on the premise that because different languages organize information differently, students need to be shown how to organize information in English if they are to write effective essays in English. Beyond that, students also need to understand that good writing is not necessarily a natural gift. It is a network of complex skills that can be taught, practiced, and mastered. The text teaches competency in these skills by taking students on a step-by-step progression through the processes that promote good writing.

The first four chapters of *Ready to Write More* comprise an overview of the building blocks of good writing: prewriting, the elements of paragraph writing, revising and editing, and the basics of essay writing. Chapters 5–9 present practice in writing five-paragraph essays of process, division and classification, causes and effects, comparison/contrast, and problem/solution. We recognize that many essays do not conform to the five-paragraph format but believe that it is helpful to students in that it gives them a structure that they can always fall back on. In Chapters 10 and 11, students practice writing summaries and expressing their opinions, both of which are necessary for Chapter 12, in which they complete a sample application form and write essays for undergraduate and graduate school applications.

The activities in *Ready to Write More* are intended to help students become competent, independent writers by engaging them in the process of writing and by encouraging them to explore and organize their ideas in writing. Students are called upon to write often and on a broad range of meaningful, thought-provoking, and interesting topics. The tasks are presented in a clear, straightforward manner and lend themselves to ease of instruction. Incorporated into the tasks is a variety of follow-up personal- and peer-revision activities. Although *Ready to Write More* is a writing book, students practice their reading, speaking, listening, and analytical skills as they progress through the text.

THE SECOND EDITION

The Second Edition features

- updated presentation of the steps of the writing process to ***prewriting, writing,*** and ***revising and editing***
- more guided practice in each step of the writing process, including more practice on writing ***thesis statements***
- updated ***model paragraphs*** and ***essays***
- ***peer-editing worksheets***
- ***Web-based exercises***

Two popular features from the First Edition, "You Be the Editor" and "On Your Own," appear regularly throughout *Ready to Write More*. "You Be the Editor" provides effective practice in error correction and proofreading to help students monitor their own errors, especially those of the type presented in Chapter 3, Revising and Editing. An answer key is included for these exercises. "On Your Own" provides students with further individual practice in the skills they have learned. In the first four chapters of the text are "Chapter Highlights," a review section that crystallizes for students the key points they will need to keep in mind as they work through the rest of the book.

We hope that you and your students enjoy working through this text now that they are *ready to write more*.

KLB and CBR

PART 1

THE ELEMENTS OF GOOD WRITING

Not everyone is a naturally gifted writer. Writing is a skill that can be practiced and mastered. In many ways, it is like driving a car. If you have ever driven in another country, you know that some of the rules of the road may be different. Just as the rules for driving differ from country to country, the conventions for writing may change from language to language.

Writing in a different language involves more than mastering its vocabulary and grammar. Language, including written language, is a reflection of the thought patterns of native speakers. In order to write well in a different language, it is important to understand the way native speakers of that language organize their thoughts. That is why it rarely works to write something in your native language and then translate it into English. The words may be in English, but the logic, organization, and thought patterns reflect those of your native language.

To write effectively in English, you must conform to the accepted patterns of organization. Practicing these patterns will put you on the road to becoming a better writer.

CHAPTER 1

Getting Ready to Write

Determining Your Attitude Toward Writing

Your attitude toward anything that you do in life greatly affects your success in doing it. Writing is no exception. Think about your attitude toward writing **in your native language** as you complete the following exercises.

A. Circle the appropriate responses to the following statements about writing in your own language.

Use the following scale:

1 = Strongly Agree   2 = Agree   3 = Neutral

4 = Disagree   5 = Strongly Disagree

a.   I enjoy keeping a diary. 1 2 3 4 5

b.   I like to write letters to my family and friends. 1 2 3 4 5

c.   Writing about my feelings helps me relax. 1 2 3 4 5

d.   I enjoy working on reports for school and work. 1 2 3 4 5

e.   I enjoy writing personal essays. 1 2 3 4 5

f.   I like to write poems, stories, or songs. 1 2 3 4 5

g.   I enjoy using e-mail. 1 2 3 4 5

h.   I like to write for my school or town newspaper. 1 2 3 4 5

i.   Writing is a creative outlet for me. 1 2 3 4 5

j.   I feel good about my writing ability. 1 2 3 4 5

Add up the numbers for each of your answers and put that number in the box.

B. Take the number from the box on page 2 and divide it by ten. The final number is your average score for the ten questions. Overall, it will tell you how much you like to write. The closer your score is to "1," the more you like to write. The closer your score is to "5," the less you like to write.

C. Based on your answers, what general conclusions can you make about your attitude toward writing in your native language?

_____

_____

_____

D. Write a paragraph about your general attitude toward writing.

READY TO WRITE

_____

_____

_____

_____

_____

_____

_____

Small-Group Discussion

In small groups discuss your main ideas from the paragraph you wrote above (number 4), and then answer the following questions.

1. What kinds of things do you enjoy writing about?
2. What kinds of writing do you think will be required in university classes?
3. What types of writing does your job or future profession require?
4. What do you hope to gain from this course?

Elements of Good Writing: SPA

SPA is an acronym that stands for **subject, purpose,** and **audience**—three of the most important elements of good writing.

You will find it easier to write if you have
- a **subject** that you know well and understand.
- a clear **purpose** for writing.
- an **audience** that you have identified.

Keeping these three elements in mind will help your writing stay focused.

SUBJECT

In order to write well, it is helpful to choose a topic that interests you and that you know and understand. If you are assigned a subject, try to find an angle or focus of that subject that you find interesting and want to explore. You will usually have to go through a process of narrowing down the general subject until you find an appropriate topic.

ENTERTAINMENT
Concerts
ROCK MUSIC
The Rolling Stones
World Tour

In the next example, the same general subject, *entertainment,* has been narrowed down to the *silent film era*.

ENTERTAINMENT
The Movies
MOVIE HISTORY
Early History
Silent Film Era

Finding a Subject

Go through the process of narrowing down each of the following general subjects until you find a specific angle that you would be interested in writing about.

TELEVISION PROGRAMS

_____

_____

_____

_____

INVENTIONS

_____

_____

_____

_____

Write a few narrowed topics on the chalkboard. Different students will probably have very different topics. Discuss and compare the various topics with your classmates.

PURPOSE

Whenever you write something, it is important to think about your purpose. To determine your purpose, you should ask yourself the question, "Why am I writing?" The three most common purposes for writing are **to entertain, to inform,** and **to persuade.** However, these three purposes are not always mutually exclusive. It is possible for a piece of writing to accomplish several purposes at the same time. For example, an article may be amusing but also educational and/or persuasive.

Identifying Purpose

A. Read each of the following selections and decide whether the author's purpose is to entertain, to inform, or to persuade. Some selections may have more than one purpose. Write your answer on the line.

> *E*l Niño is the name given to an unusual warming of the Pacific Ocean that can cause weather changes all over the world. El Niño has troubled much of the world with disruptive weather for several years now, but researchers at the National Oceanic and Atmospheric Administration announced yesterday that El Niño's strength has decreased. Long-range climate forecasts for events like El Niño can help farmers successfully choose which crops to plant. Forecasts in Peru, for example, have helped increase the nation's overall economic product by preventing millions of dollars' worth of crop losses.

Selection 1: _____

> "Photography is art," says Saundra Lane. She is a trustee of the Museum of Fine Arts in Boston and a photo collector. She says that whether or not photography is art was a debatable point until the 1970s. All that changed when one of Ansel Adams's photographs was chosen for the cover of *Time* magazine. Ever since, the value of photography as an art form has no longer been open to question. Exhibitions of the works of great photographers are now regularly featured in museum shows the world over.

Selection 2: _____

There was a faith healer named Deal
Who said, "Although pain isn't real,
If I sit on a pin, and I puncture my skin
I dislike what I think that I feel!"

(author unknown)

Selection 3: _____

The president is due in Atlanta on February 13 for a campaign fund-raising dinner, the White House said yesterday. The president is expected to arrive in Atlanta aboard his private plane, *Air Force One*, after giving a speech at the Department of Health and Human Services in Washington, D.C. He will return to the White House later that night.

Selection 4: _____

It has been said that there is no love more sincere than the love of good food.
You will surely agree when you join us for dinner at

The Atelier
in the heart of Soho.

Our highly acclaimed chef will attend to your every whim and fancy as you choose from our impressive menu of fine French cuisine, artfully prepared, presented, and served in our tastefully decorated restaurant.

Whether you're in New York for a special occasion or not, we'll make this occasion special. You'll fall in love.

Selection 5: _____

Renting a car offers many attractive advantages to the traveler: independence, convenience, dependability, and a sudden, massive lowering of the IQ. I know what I'm talking about here. I live in Miami, and every winter we have a huge infestation of rental-car drivers, who come down here seeking warm weather and the opportunity to make sudden left turns without signaling, across six lanes of traffic, into convenience stores. My wife and I have affectionately nicknamed these people "Alamos," because so many of them seem to get their cars from Alamo, which evidently requires that every driver leave several major brain lobes as a deposit. We're tempted to stay off the highways altogether during tourist season, just stockpile food and spend the entire winter huddled in our bedrooms, but we're not sure we'd be safe *there*.

Source: *Dave Barry's Only Travel Guide You'll Ever Need*, by Dave Barry

Selection 6: _____

B. Complete the chart below by putting each type of writing in the appropriate box. Some types of writing may go in more than one box.

plays	jokes	newspaper articles
memos	stories	novels
songs	comparisons	letters
essays	editorials	textbooks
poetry	analyses	instructions

ENTERTAIN	INFORM	PERSUADE

C. Look through your local newspaper and find one example of writing that entertains, one that informs, and one that persuades. Bring your articles to class to share with your classmates.

1. Which kind of article (entertaining, informational, or persuasive) was the easiest to find?

_____

_____

2. Which kind was the most difficult to find? Why?

_____

_____

3. Which kind of writing do you think students are usually asked to do?

_____

_____

AUDIENCE

What you write about (subject) and your reason for writing (purpose) are greatly affected by whom you are writing for (audience). Because you will usually be writing for an audience, you will communicate your ideas more effectively if you keep that audience in mind. Remember that all audiences have expectations, but those expectations vary from one audience to another.

As you work through this book, your audience will usually be your teacher or classmates. However, you will occasionally be asked to write with another audience in mind. This will give you practice in choosing the appropriate words and varying your tone.

Read the following two e-mails and notice the difference in tone.

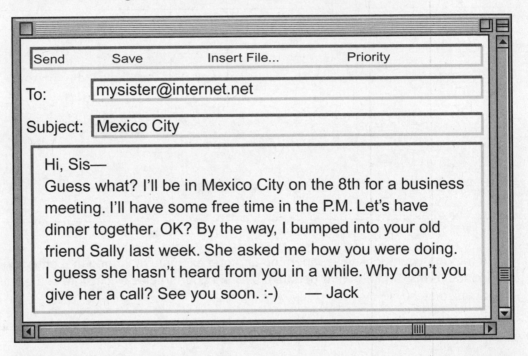

Send   Save   Insert File...   Priority

To: mysister@internet.net

Subject: Mexico City

Hi, Sis—
Guess what? I'll be in Mexico City on the 8th for a business meeting. I'll have some free time in the P.M. Let's have dinner together. OK? By the way, I bumped into your old friend Sally last week. She asked me how you were doing. I guess she hasn't heard from you in a while. Why don't you give her a call? See you soon. :-)   — Jack

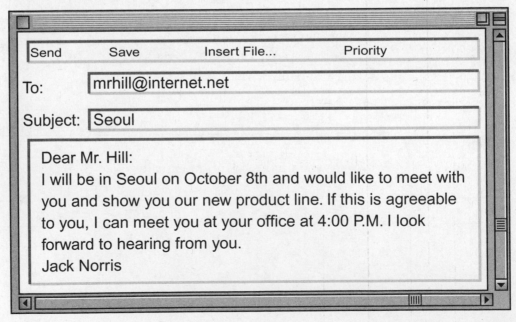

Send   Save   Insert File...   Priority

To: mrhill@internet.net

Subject: Seoul

Dear Mr. Hill:
I will be in Seoul on October 8th and would like to meet with you and show you our new product line. If this is agreeable to you, I can meet you at your office at 4:00 P.M. I look forward to hearing from you.
Jack Norris

In small groups, make a list of the differences between the two e-mails. Which one uses more formal language? Which one is more conversational?

1. _____

2. _____

3. _____

4. _____

Writing for Different Audiences

A letter you would write to your best friend asking him or her to lend you some money would be quite different from a letter to a bank loan officer. The two letters would probably include different expressions and have a different tone.

A. On a separate piece of paper, write a letter to your best friend asking to borrow money.

B. Then write a letter to the loan officer at a bank asking to borrow money.

C. Compare your two letters and answer the following questions.

1. Which letter was easier for you to write? Why?
2. In which letter did you use a more formal style?

DETERMINING SUBJECT, PURPOSE, AND AUDIENCE

Choose one of the following general subjects to write a paragraph about.

- your hometown
- your school
- your family

After you have chosen your subject, decide on a specific focus that interests you. Then determine your purpose and identify your audience.

Subject: _____

Focus: _____

Purpose: _____

Audience: _____

Finally, write your paragraph.

_____

_____

_____

_____

_____

_____

_____

_____

Now find another focus of the same subject that you want to explore. Choose a different purpose for your writing and pick another audience.

Subject: _____

Focus: _____

Purpose: _____

Audience:_____

Write a second paragraph.

_____

_____

_____

_____

_____

_____

_____

_____

How are your two paragraphs alike? How are they different?

The Writing Process

Very few people pick up a pen or sit down at a computer and produce a perfect piece of writing on the first try. Most writers spend a lot of time thinking before they write and then work through a series of steps while they are composing. The final product is often the result of several careful revisions. It takes patience as well as skill to write well. You should think of writing as a process involving the following steps:

Step One: Prewriting

generating ideas, planning, and organizing your ideas

↓

Step Two: Writing

using your ideas to write a first draft

↓

Step Three: Revising and Editing

improving what you have written

In this and the next two chapters, you will learn more about these three steps and practice them.

Step One: Prewriting

For many people, the hardest part of writing is *getting started*. Whether you enjoy writing or not, you will find it easier to write if you do some prewriting exercises to get started. Prewriting is a way to warm up your brain before you write, just as you warm up your car's engine before you drive.

GENERATING IDEAS

Following are several prewriting techniques that writers use to generate ideas. Some of the most popular methods are *brainstorming, clustering, freewriting,* and *keeping a journal*.

Brainstorming

Brainstorming is a quick way to generate a lot of ideas on a subject. The purpose is to come up with a list of as many ideas as possible without worrying about how you will use them. Your list may include words, phrases, sentences, or even questions. To brainstorm, follow these steps:

1. Begin with a broad topic.
2. Write down as many associations as you can in ten minutes.
3. Add more items to your list by answering the questions *what, how, when, where, why,* and *who*.
4. Group the items on the list that go together.
5. Cross out items that do not belong.

Your list may seem very unfocused as you are working on it. But you will later go back and organize the items on your list and decide which ones you want to include in your essay and which you want to discard.

The following is an example of brainstorming on the general subject of *superstitions*.

TOPIC: SUPERSTITIONS	
Friday 13th	eat scrambled eggs for breakfast on day
breaking a mirror	of a game
always wear pearl necklace for tests	don't walk under ladders
look for four-leaf clovers	don't step on cracks
don't stay on 13th floor in a hotel	wear green when I fly
sit in center of room for tests	use lucky shoelaces in tennis shoes
wear lucky T-shirt for games	switch watch to right wrist for tests
finding a penny	never start a trip on Friday

In this example, after the author made her list, she read it over, and decided to write an essay that focused on her personal superstitions. She grouped together similar ideas and eliminated items that did not fit in. In the end, she grouped her list into three categories covering superstitions about *school*, *travel*, and *sports*.

SCHOOL:	SPORTS:
always wear pearl necklace for tests	wear lucky T-shirt for games
sit in center of room for tests	use lucky shoelaces in tennis shoes
switch watch to right wrist for tests	eat scrambled eggs for breakfast on
TRAVEL:	day of a game
never start a trip on Friday	
don't stay on 13th floor in a hotel	
wear green when I fly	

Practicing Brainstorming

In the space below, brainstorm a list of ideas for the general topic of *travel.*

Now, group similar ideas together and eliminate ones that do not fit in.

Clustering

If you prefer to work with information visually, clustering might be a good technique for you. Clustering is a visual way of generating ideas. It is a technique to show you the connections among your ideas using circles and lines. To cluster, follow these steps:

1. Write your topic in the center of a piece of paper and draw a circle around it.
2. Think about your topic and write any ideas that come to mind in circles around the main circle.
3. Connect these ideas to the center circle with a line.
4. Think about each of your new ideas, write more related ideas in circles around them, and connect them to their corresponding ideas with a line.
5. Repeat this process until you run out of ideas.

On the next page is an example of a cluster diagram on the topic of *cars.* In this example, what topic or topics would the author probably choose to write about? Why?

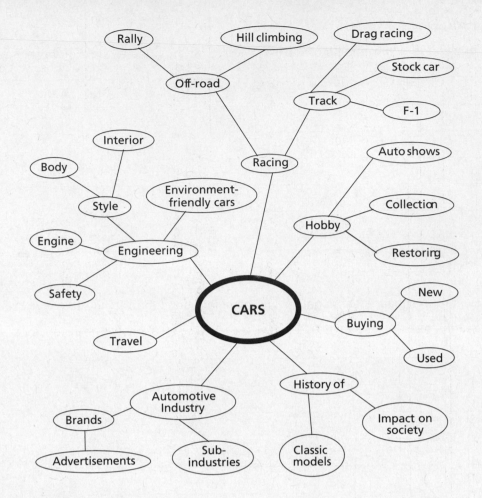

Practicing Clustering

Use the space below to practice clustering for an essay on the topic of *music.*

Freewriting

If you have a hard time finding a focus for a broad subject, freewriting might be a helpful technique for you. Freewriting is writing as much as you can, as fast as you can, without worrying about mistakes. To freewrite, follow these steps:

1. Write your general topic at the top of your page.
2. Start writing, and write as much as you can, as fast as you can, for ten minutes.
3. Don't stop for any reason. Don't worry if your mind wanders away from your original idea. Don't worry about mistakes. Just keep writing. You can go back later and revise. Let your ideas flow.
4. If you can't think of anything, write "my mind is blank, my mind is blank," or something similar, over and over again until a new thought comes into your mind.
5. Read your freewriting and see if there are any ideas you can develop into a paragraph.

Read the freewriting sample below on the topic of *computers*.

Computers

I love computers. They make my life so much easier than it was when I had to use a typewriter every time I wanted to type something. Back then I had to start all over again whenever I made a mistake. I really don't understand computers very well. Whenever I have a problem, I have to get someone else to help me. I'm always afraid to try to fix it myself. I guess I'm computer-phobic. My mind just went blank. It went blank. It went blank. Just like my computer screen does when I have a problem. And I have so many problems with my computer. There are always technical problems with computers. The whole world worries about technical problems. They are so unpredictable and unreliable. What else can I say about computers? I only use them for word processing and e-mail. I enjoy communicating with my friends by e-mail. That's all. I know there are lots of other uses but I'll never get involved in them. I don't understand computers.

When you freewrite, your mind may jump around as new ideas come into it. You can see that as this author was writing, new and different ideas came into his mind. In the example above, there are several different ideas that could be developed into paragraphs. List some of them below.

_____

_____

_____

Compare your list with a classmate's. Did you include the same items?

Practicing Freewriting

Write for ten minutes on the subject of *your plans for the future.* Your teacher will tell you when to begin and when to stop writing.

_____

_____

_____

_____

_____

_____

_____

_____

_____

_____

_____

_____

_____

_____

Did you generate any ideas that you could now write a paragraph about? If so, what are they?

_____

_____

_____

Keeping a Journal

Some people find that keeping a journal is helpful. When you are not given a specific subject to write on, you can refer to your journal for possible topics. If you decide to keep a journal, start by buying a notebook and writing in it for a few minutes every day. Use the time to write about anything you want. For example, you could write about the events of your day, the people you met or talked to, or your reaction to something that you heard, read, or saw.

Use your journal as a record of your daily thoughts and activities, as a means of self-expression, or as a way of understanding yourself better. No matter what your original reason for keeping a journal, you will find it a valuable source of material in your future writing and thinking.

Here is an example of a journal entry.

November 19

    I just got back from an ice hockey game. Ray had an extra ticket and asked me if I wanted it. The Boston Bruins beat the St. Louis Blues 5–2. Our seats were really high up, almost to the roof, but we could still see more than if we had watched it on television. It's so much easier to see the puck when you are there than when you watch a game on TV. I started talking to the old man sitting next to me about hockey in "the good old days." He went to his first hockey game in 1939—the game when the Bruins won the Stanley Cup World Championship! He talked on and on about the changes he has seen in the kinds of equipment, rules, and the style of play since his day. He remembers when players weren't required to wear helmets, but he said that the play was less rough back then. There weren't as many fights. I wonder if that's really true. Hockey has always been a pretty physical game, and I bet emotions have always run high among the players. It was a good game. I hope Ray can get me tickets to more games this season. It looks like the Bruins might be good this year.

List several of the general topics from this journal entry that the author might use to develop a paragraph.

_____

_____

_____

Compare your list with a classmate's. Did you include the same items?

Writing a Journal Entry

Use the journal page below to write your first journal entry. Write about something that happened to you recently.

PLANNING

Part of prewriting is planning and organizing your ideas. Making a simple outline of the ideas you generated from prewriting will help you organize your thoughts as you plan your paragraph. You can use your outline as a guide and refer to it while you are composing.

Here is an example of an outline based on the ideas generated from brainstorming on the topic *superstitions*. Notice that the three headings in this outline are the same three categories determined in the brainstorming exercise.

TOPIC: MY SUPERSTITIONS

1. Superstitions about school
   a. always wear pearl necklace for tests
   b. sit in center of room for tests
   c. switch watch to right wrist for tests
2. Superstitions about travel
   a. don't stay on 13th floor in a hotel
   b. never start a trip on Friday
   c. wear green when I fly

3. Superstitions about sports
   a. wear lucky T-shirt for games
   b. use lucky shoelaces in tennis shoes
   c. eat scrambled eggs for breakfast on day of a game

Making a Simple Outline

A. Prepare an outline based on the groups of similar ideas you created in the brainstorming exercise about *travel* on page 13.

Topic: Travel

_____   _____

_____   _____

_____   _____

_____   _____

_____   _____

_____   _____

B. Prepare an outline based on the topics in your clustering diagram on *music* on page 14.

Topic: Music

_____   _____

_____   _____

_____   _____

_____   _____

_____   _____

_____   _____

_____   _____

Chapter Highlights

1. List and explain the three things you should consider when you write something.

_____

_____

_____

2. What are the three basic steps in the writing process?

_____

_____

_____

3. What are four common prewriting techniques you learned about in this chapter?

_____

_____

_____

_____

4. What is one way you can organize the ideas you generated from prewriting?

_____

CHAPTER 2

Writing Paragraphs

After you have spent some time thinking about your topic and doing the necessary prewriting, you are ready for the next step in the writing process: writing your paragraph.

Step Two: Writing

When you write the first draft of your paragraph, use the ideas you generated from prewriting and your outline as a guide.

PARAGRAPH BASICS

Most writing that is longer than a few sentences is organized into paragraphs. A **paragraph** is a group of sentences that all relate to a single topic. Paragraphs can include many different kinds of information and serve different purposes. For example, some paragraphs describe people or places. Other paragraphs explain how to do or make something, narrate a series of events, compare or contrast two things, or describe causes and effects.

PARTS OF A PARAGRAPH

Remember that a paragraph is a group of sentences about one topic. The topic of the paragraph is usually stated in the first sentence. This sentence is called the *topic sentence*. The other sentences add details to the topic. They are called *supporting sentences*. Some paragraphs also have a *concluding sentence*, which summarizes the ideas of the paragraph. It is the last sentence of the paragraph.

Here is an example of a paragraph based on the outline about superstitions on page 19.

TOPIC SENTENCE — Superstitions affect several aspects of my life. First of all, I have a lot of superstitions about school, especially tests. For example, I always wear the pearl necklace that my grandmother gave me when I have to take a test. I think it brings me good luck, and I am afraid that I will do poorly if I forget to wear it. When I get to school, I always find a seat right in the middle of the room, sit down, and then switch my watch to my right wrist before the test begins. In addition, I am  very superstitious about traveling. I will never start a trip on a Friday because I am sure it will bring me bad luck. When I have to stay in a hotel, I refuse to sleep in a room on the 13th floor. For me, 13 is an unlucky number. In addition, I always wear something green, my lucky color, on the first day of a trip. Finally, like many other athletes, I am especially superstitious when it comes to my sport, tennis. When I dress for a match, I always wear the same white T-shirt with my initials on it. I also use the same shoelaces in my sneakers that I have had since I first started playing tennis. As soon as I buy a new pair of sneakers, the first thing I do is replace the laces with my lucky ones. I am also superstitious about my breakfast on the day of a match. I always eat the same thing: eggs and a muffin. All in all, I am superstitious about many aspects of my life.

SUPPORTING SENTENCES (margin label)

CONCLUDING SENTENCE (margin label)

Notice that this paragraph also contains the following important features:

- The first sentence is indented.
- The first word of every sentence is capitalized.
- Each sentence ends with a period.

As you draft your paragraph, remember that you need to do several things:

1. **State your point in a topic sentence.**
2. **Support your point.**
3. **Develop a single focus.**
4. **Organize sentences logically and add transitions.**

State Your Point in a Topic Sentence

When you write a paragraph in English, the most important thing you need to do is to express your main point. This should be written in one clear sentence, *the topic sentence*. The rest of the paragraph must develop and support the point you made in the topic sentence.

The topic sentence is usually the first sentence of a paragraph. It is the most important one in your paragraph because it controls all the other sentences. It states the topic (main idea) and the **focus** (main emphasis) of the paragraph. You can think of the topic sentence as being in control of the whole paragraph. In this way, a topic sentence functions like a traffic sign controlling vehicles on the road. It shows readers which way they are going, just as a traffic sign helps direct drivers.

> A good topic sentence
> - states the **topic** of the paragraph.
> - identifies the **focus.**

Look at these two topic sentences.

A. Nuclear power is our greatest hope for solving the energy crisis.

   1. What is the topic of this sentence?

   _____

   2. What is the focus?

   _____

B. Nuclear power is a huge threat to life on the planet.

   1. What is the topic of this sentence?

   _____

   2. What is the focus?

   _____

Notice that both sentences have the same topic, but the focus is different.

Analyzing Topic Sentences

For each statement below, underline the topic and draw a circle around the focus.

   1. Mahatma Gandhi was an influential leader.

   2. E-mail is a great way to stay in touch with your family and friends.

   3. The clothes we wear often reflect a lot about our personality.

   4. The Japanese subway system is very efficient.

   5. Television commercials are often insulting to women.

   6. My older brother is a perfectionist.

   7. The laws on child abuse should be strictly enforced.

   8. Being a twin has both advantages and disadvantages.

   9. The new shopping mall has brought many economic benefits to our community.

   10. Golf is a difficult sport to master.

A good topic sentence should not be too general or too specific. If a topic sentence is too general, you will not be able to support the topic in one paragraph. If it is too specific, you won't have enough to write about in the rest of the paragraph.

Look at the following topic sentences. One is too general, and the other is too specific.

Swimming is fun.

This statement is too general to be developed adequately into one paragraph. There is too much to say about the topic.

I swim laps for 30 minutes every morning.

This statement is too specific to be developed into a paragraph. There isn't enough to say about the topic.

Now look at this topic sentence. It would be easy to support this sentence in one paragraph. It is not too general or too specific.

Exercising every morning has several positive effects on my health.

Evaluating Topic Sentences

Work with a partner. Read the following statements and put a checkmark next to the three that you think are effective topic sentences. Draw a line through the sentences that are not good topic sentences because they are either too general or too specific. Rewrite those sentences on a separate piece of paper. Discuss the improved topic sentences with your partner.

_____ 1. My round-trip plane ticket to Ankara, Turkey, cost over $950.

_____ 2. The topic of this paragraph is learning new things.

_____ 3. American music reflects the native music of many of its immigrant groups.

_____ 4. Everyone needs a hobby.

_____ 5. American music is the subject of this paragraph.

_____ 6. The first published collection of African-American music, *Slave Songs of the United States*, appeared in 1867.

_____ 7. Vacations are expensive.

_____ 8. Russian is a difficult language to learn.

_____ 9. Learning how to write in English can be a frustrating experience for many foreign students.

_____ 10. The Chinese language has over 50,000 characters.

Writing Topic Sentences

Write a topic sentence for each of the paragraphs below. Be sure that each one states the main point and focus.

Example:

The customs associated with giving gifts vary from country to country.

Whether you are a tourist, a student, or a businessperson, it is important to know the gift-giving customs of the country you are visiting. For example, if you are invited for dinner, flowers are a safe and appreciated gift throughout the world. In much of Europe, however, red roses symbolize romance and would be inappropriate. In Austria and Germany, it is considered bad luck to receive an even number of flowers. If you are in Hong Kong, gifts to avoid are clocks, which symbolize death, and scissors or knives, which indicate the end of the relationship. In Japan, you can impress your hosts by paying attention to the Japanese rules for gift-giving: Always wrap the gift, but not in white paper, as white symbolizes death. In addition, never give four of anything, since the Japanese word for the number four is also the word for death. As in Korea and much of Asia, do not expect your gift to be opened until after you have left. In the Middle East, be careful about admiring one of your host's possessions. He or she may offer it to you and would be insulted if you refused it. No matter where in the world you are, you will feel more comfortable if you take the time to learn some of the local gift-giving customs.

Source: *Dos and Taboos Around the World*

1. _There are some reasons that pets become our good friends._ _people keeps pets for a variety of reasons._

Most often, they keep them for pleasure and companionship. In fact, many people consider their pet to be part of the family. In addition to their value as loved and loving companions, pets serve practical purposes, such as protecting homes and property, destroying insects, and even providing means of transportation. They may also serve as emotional outlets for the elderly or the childless. Recently, the benefit of pet-facilitated psychotherapy has been demonstrated. Finally, some people keep pets for their beauty or rarity or, in the case of birds, for their songs.

Source: *Encarta*

2. _Climate affects our life environment_ _(concerns)_

For instance, climate affects the kinds of clothes we wear and even the colors we choose to wear. Since it affects the kinds of crops we can grow successfully, it influences our eating habits. Architecture is also affected by climate. Engineers and architects must think about climate when they make decisions about the construction, materials, design, and style of buildings. Even our choices in transportation are determined by the climate in which we live. Climate also plays a big part in economic development. A climate that is too hot, too cold, or too dry makes farming, industry, and transportation difficult and slows down economic development.

3. *Chronobiologists, scientists studies some time simptoms.*
of the time

Symptoms may last for one day or several days and vary greatly in severity. Chronobiologists, scientists who study the effects of time on living things, say that the seriousness of your reaction depends on several factors. One factor is the number of time zones you crossed. Your jet lag will probably be worse if you crossed several time zones. Another factor is whether you flew east to west or west to east. It is easier to adjust after an east-to-west flight. Personality factors also affect how easily you adapt to the new time. For example, "night" people adapt more easily than "morning" people. Extroverts adjust more easily than introverts. Flexible people who don't mind changes have fewer problems than inflexible people who are rigid and don't like change. Younger people suffer less than older people. Finally, healthier people usually get over jet lag more easily than people who are sick.

4. _____

For example, hardware stores sold half a million shovels last winter. This was up 75 percent from the year before. Customers also bought 50 million pounds of rock salt, which is used to melt ice. Ice scrapers were another "hot" item. Service stations reported that sales of ice scrapers in December, January, and February equaled sales of the past four years combined. Finally, sales of winter clothes were higher than ever. For example, hat sales were up 13 percent, and retailers sold about 95 million pairs of gloves. Stores that usually sell 150,000 pairs of winter boots sold over 350,000 pairs.

Write several topic sentences on the board to compare and discuss.

Support Your Point

After you have stated your point in the topic sentence, you need to support it with reasons, facts, and examples. As a writer, it is your job to provide enough support to prove the point you made in your topic sentence. Your supporting sentences should be as specific as possible. Supporting sentences that are vague or that merely repeat the point you made in the topic sentence are not effective.

Analyzing Paragraphs for Support

Look at the following two paragraphs. Both begin with the topic sentence *Our family trip to Costa Rica last summer was very exciting,* but only one develops it with enough specific support. Choose the paragraph that you think provides enough specific support. Underline examples of specific support.

Paragraph 1
topic   *focus*

Our family trip to Costa Rica last summer was very exciting. Every day we saw something new and different. One day we went hiking, which was really an incredible experience. Another day we took a rafting trip down a river. We saw lots of unusual plants and animals that we had never seen before. We did many things that we will never forget. Everyone agreed that this was the best trip we have ever taken.

Paragraph 2

Our family trip to Costa Rica last summer was very exciting. We were there for two weeks, and not a day went by without something unusual happening. On our second day, a boa constrictor swam right in front of us while we were rafting down the Río Claro. Another day, spider monkeys threw branches at us deep in the rain forest. Hiking on the primitive trails in Corcovado National Park, we saw brilliant scarlet macaws and toucans with huge yellow beaks. Whenever we look at the pictures from our trip, we all agree that it was the most exciting one we have ever taken.

Evaluating Support

Read the following sets of paragraphs and answer the questions. Each paragraph begins with a clear topic sentence, but only one paragraph in each set develops the main point with adequate support.

Set 1

Paragraph 1

The repairs on my car were much more expensive than I had anticipated. When I saw the final bill, I was in shock. It was twice as much as I had planned on. I had to pay $395 to get the brakes repaired and another $100 to get the wheels aligned. The engine oil change was $30, and the replacement of the air filter was another $20.

Paragraph 2

The repairs on my car were much more expensive than I had anticipated. The mechanic did a good job, but I think I was overcharged for everything. I never imagined that the final bill would be so high. In fact, I had to borrow some money from my friend to pay it. The next time my car needs repairs, I'll go to a different garage.

1. Which paragraph provides more specific support?

   _____

2. What four supporting details does the author include in that paragraph?

   _____   _____

   _____   _____

Set 2

Paragraph 1

My chemistry course is very difficult and time consuming. The professor doesn't seem to realize that chemistry isn't the only course we're taking. He gives lots of homework and too much reading. The worst thing is that his lectures are really boring. I'm not interested in chemistry, so I hate reading the textbook. I know I'm not the only student complaining about this course.

Paragraph 2

My chemistry course is very difficult and time consuming. First of all, we're responsible for two labs every week, which means a minimum of ten hours a week in the lab. To make matters worse, the professor gives at least three tests per month. The questions are very tricky, and we have to memorize long, complicated formulas. Finally, the reading load is also quite heavy—as much as twenty-five pages a night. I often spend all my free time doing the required reading.

1. Which paragraph provides more specific support?

   _____

2. What four supporting details does the author include in that paragraph?

   _____   _____

   _____   _____

Set 3

Paragraph 1 *It says How does it destroy the the environment*

In my opinion, the effects of global warming on the environment could be disastrous. For one thing, deserts will become hotter and drier and continue to expand. Rising seas, caused in part by the melting of half the world's mountain glaciers, will flood low-lying islands and coasts, threatening millions of people. Global warming will change the climate regionally and globally, altering natural vegetation and affecting crop production. Indeed, all kinds of plants and forests, from the tropics to the Arctic tundra, will undergo radical transformation. Finally, higher temperatures could also cause more extreme storms, allowing tropical diseases to invade temperate areas.

Paragraph 2 *1   2+3   what*

In my opinion, a warming of the atmosphere would have serious environmental effects. Something needs to be done about this. Once it begins, the trend toward warmer temperatures could be disastrous. It would speed up the melting of ice caps and raise sea levels. An increase in atmospheric carbon dioxide of 10 percent over the past century has led some authorities to predict a long-term warming of the Earth's climate. This warming could have a severe impact on our environment and the world as we know it. In 1992, over 150 nations signed a treaty to reduce the emission of gases that intensify the greenhouse effect and result in global warming and then in 1997 met in Kyoto, Japan, to discuss it further. Since global warming would probably have a negative effect on our environment, I hope all nations take the treaty seriously.

1. Which paragraph is vague, repetitive, and lacks enough support to prove the point?

   _____

2. Which sentences in that paragraph simply restate the topic?

   _____

   _____

3. Which sentences are true but do not really support the point that global warming could have a profound effect on the environment?

   _____

   _____

   _____

   _____

Stay on topic
Repeat the topic and

Practice Writing Supporting Sentences

Write three supporting sentences for each of the following topic sentences.

Example:

I am terrible at doing the laundry.

a. _I forget to separate the colored clothes from the white ones and sometimes end up with gray underwear._

b. _I rarely read the cleaning instructions and have ruined clothes by putting them in the washing machine instead of dry cleaning them._

c. _I often shrink my favorite shirts because I leave them in the dryer for too long._

1. I love eating food from different countries.

   a. _____

   b. _____

   c. _____

2. Summer is my favorite season.

   a. _____

   b. _____

   c. _____

3. There is too much violence on television.

   a. _____

   b. _____

   c. _____

4. There are several ways to conserve electricity.

   a. _____

   b. _____

   c. _____

5. It is almost impossible to study in my dormitory.

   a. _____

   b. _____

   c. _____

Choose the topic sentence that you have the best support for and develop it into a paragraph.

_____

_____

_____

_____

_____

_____

_____

_____

_____

_____

_____

_____

Exchange paragraphs with a partner. Does your partner's topic sentence have enough support? If not, give suggestions for adding support.

Supplying Specific Details

To write a fully developed paragraph, you will often need to provide specific details to strengthen your main supporting points. Each of the following paragraphs has a topic sentence and three or four main supporting points. With a classmate, complete the paragraphs by adding your own specific details to clarify each supporting point.

1.   My mother nags me constantly. For one thing, my room is never clean enough to suit her. _Although I hang up my clothes once a week, she expects me to put them away every night before I go to bed. She also hates it if I leave any food, wrappers, or soda cans in my room._ In addition, she never thinks I've spent enough time on my schoolwork. _____

_____

_____

_____ Finally, she is always telling me to improve my appearance. _____

_____

_____

2.   After my grandfather moved in with us, I began to realize the benefits of
living with an older person. First of all, he has told me a lot of stories about
our family history. _____

_____

_____

_____ Since my grandfather is retired, he has been
able to spend a lot of time helping me with my schoolwork. _____

_____

_____

_____ Most importantly, I've
learned to appreciate the special qualities an older person can have. _____

_____

_____

3.   There are many ways to economize on a trip to _____
and still have a good time. First, you can shop around for the best airfare. ____

_____

_____

_____ Once you get there, you do not need to stay in the most
expensive hotels. _____

_____

_____

You can also economize on food. _____

_____

_____

_____ Finally, you should take advantage of all the free
cultural and historical offerings. _____

_____

_____

Develop a Single Focus

In addition to a clear topic sentence and adequate support, a good paragraph must have a single focus. When every sentence contributes to the main idea, the paragraph has a single focus. If a sentence does not relate to the main idea, you should eliminate it.

Analyzing Paragraphs for Single Focus

A. Read the next two paragraphs. Notice that the first one has a single focus because all the sentences relate to the topic sentence, but the second one includes some information that does not relate to the main idea.

Paragraph 1

My apartment is in a terrible location. First of all, it is too far away from the important stores and services. It is several miles from a grocery store, bank, post office, library, or pharmacy. To make matters worse, there is no convenient public transportation in my neighborhood. The one bus line near my apartment runs only one bus an hour and has a very limited route. Almost everywhere I need to go involves changing buses and takes a lot of time. In addition, my apartment is in a high-crime area. Gangs of teenagers roam the streets, threatening the neighbors. Last month alone, eight robberies took place on our block. The elderly woman who lives next door had her purse snatched while she was walking her dog. Finally, because my apartment is near an industrial area, the pollution is awful. A nearby chemical plant causes so much smog that it is often hard for me to breathe. I agree with people who say that when you are looking for an apartment, location is everything.

All the sentences in the first paragraph support and develop the single point stated in the topic sentence: "My apartment is in a terrible location." The paragraph has a single focus.

Paragraph 2

I love the location of my new house. For one thing, it's a very safe neighborhood, and I'm not afraid to go out alone. There's almost no crime, and most people don't even lock their doors. In addition, the neighborhood is in a convenient location. Lots of stores, schools, and restaurants are nearby. Within a few miles, there is also a library, health and fitness center, and movie theater. Most of all, I really like the people who live in this neighborhood. They're friendly and helpful and seem to want to keep our community safe and clean. My new house is roomy, comfortable, and sunny, but I need to buy some more furniture.

The focus of this paragraph is expressed in the first sentence: "I love the location of my new house." Most of the other sentences develop and support this sentence. But the last sentence, "My new house is roomy, comfortable, and sunny, but I need to buy some more furniture" has nothing to do with location. It is not related to the topic. It should NOT be included in this paragraph.

B. The topic of the following paragraph is Boston's annual New Year's Eve celebration. As you read it, decide which sentences do not belong in the paragraph because they do not support the topic sentence. Cross out the irrelevant sentences.

Every year on New Year's Eve, the city of Boston hosts a community celebration called First Night so people can celebrate the new year together. Boston was the first city in the United States to launch a special event to celebrate New Year's Eve. First Night attracts over 1.5 million people. For the $20 cost of a First Night button, people gain general admission to many different events. ~~Boston is the higher-education capital of the United States.~~ ~~The two largest universities within the city itself are Boston University and Northeastern University, and in nearby Cambridge are Harvard University and the Massachusetts Institute of Technology.~~ The evening begins with a grand costumed parade

Ice sculpture at First Night Celebration

around the Boston Common and ends at midnight with fireworks over Boston Harbor. In between, there are more than 250 performances of international music, dance, and theater, as well as puppetry and many films to choose from. ~~Boston is also host to the well-known Boston Marathon, which is run in April.~~ Two hundred cities and towns in the United States, Canada, and Australia have now launched celebrations like the one in Boston for New Year's Eve.

Which sentences did you cross out? Compare the ones you deleted with those your classmates deleted.

C. Now read the following paragraph and underline the topic sentence. Then decide if any of the sentences are irrelevant and cross them out.

If you suffer from mental or physical stress while flying, you can take several precautions to protect yourself. First of all, you might consider taking a Fearful Flier workshop. The purpose of this workshop is to help replace the myths about flying with facts, such as what makes a plane fly and how crews are trained. There are also many interesting workshops you can take to relieve stress at work. Planning ahead is a second way to cut down on stress. Leave plenty of time for your drive to the airport and have your travel agent make an advance seat assignment for you in a part of the plane you like. Many airports have shops and restaurants where you can spend time between flights. Third, communicate your fears. If the flight crew knows that a passenger is anxious, they will make more of an effort to put you at ease. Another tip is to stay loose, both physically and mentally. Wear loose, comfortable clothing and try to relax. Flex your hands and feet. Get up and walk around. Unfortunately, the food served on many flights is unappetizing. Fifth, don't allow yourself to get bored. Bring along a good book, some magazines, or a lot of absorbing work. Another precaution you can take is to drink plenty of water and fruit juices so that you don't become dehydrated from the pressurized cabin air. Dehydration is one of the most common causes of discomfort among air travelers. Last but not least, keep your ears open by swallowing, chewing gum, or talking.

Source: *Car and Travel*

Which sentences did you cross out? Compare the ones you deleted with the ones your classmates deleted.

Organize Sentences Logically and Add Transitions

Finally, a good paragraph must be easy to understand. To help readers understand your ideas, you should do two things:

- Arrange the sentences so that the order of ideas makes sense.
- Use transitions to help the reader understand how the ideas in your paragraph are connected.

Organization

The way you arrange your information depends on the kind of paragraph you are writing. For example, if you are telling a story, the logical organization of sentences will be chronological, that is, according to **time order.** If you are describing what your bedroom looks like, you will organize the details according to where they are located. In this case you will use **spatial order.** Finally, if you are discussing examples, causes, effects, or reasons, you will probably use **order of importance.** In this type of paragraph, you might begin with the least important item and end with the most important one.

Time Order	Use this method when you are telling a story, describing what happened, giving instructions, or explaining a process.
Spatial Order	Use this method when you are describing what something looks like.
Order of Importance	Use this method to organize ideas, examples, and reasons for emphasis. You can order them in various ways; for example, from least to most important, from general to specific, from most to least familiar, or from simplest to most complex (or the reverse of all of these).

Analyzing Organization

Read the following three paragraphs. Identify the method of organization used in each paragraph: time order, spatial order, or order of importance.

1.   My anthropology teacher likes a classroom layout that encourages interaction among students. He sets up the physical space so that it encourages us to interact with each other as much as possible. He likes to have his desk in the center of the room. That means that the students surround him and everyone can always see everyone else. As you walk into the room, the first thing you see is the enormous windows directly opposite the door. If you look to the left, you will see his bulletin boards, which take up the entire back wall of the room. To the right is the computer station with enough computers for ten students. Behind you as you face the windows are the chalkboards. Above the boards, ready to be rolled down whenever we need them, are many different maps of the world. This type of classroom may not work for every teacher, but it works very well for Mr. Carter.

Method of organization: _____

2.   Homing pigeons have been known to fly more than 1,600 kilometers in two days. How do they do it? Homing pigeons use a combination of navigational cues to find their way to distant places. One cue they use is the position of the sun. Using the sun as their compass, they compensate for its apparent movement, see both ultraviolet and polarized light, and employ a backup compass for cloudy days. Another navigational cue homing pigeons

use is based on their mental map of the landmarks in their home areas. Even if a pigeon is taken hundreds of kilometers from its loft in total darkness, it will depart almost directly for home when it is released. The most important cue homing pigeons use is the magnetic field of the Earth. Their magnetic compass enables homing pigeons to navigate on cloudy and foggy days.

Method of organization: _____

3. The story of the Earth's oceans begins 200 million years ago when the Earth was just a ball of hot rock. At first, its surface was covered with erupting volcanoes, which released huge amounts of gas, including a gas made up of water particles, called water vapor. Eventually the Earth cooled, causing the water vapor to turn back into liquid water and fall from the skies as torrential rain. The rain lasted for thousands and thousands of years. Finally, rainwater filled all the hollows around the Earth's surface, forming oceans and seas. Today, water covers almost three-quarters of the Earth's surface, and over 97 percent of all this water is stored in the Earth's four huge oceans: the Pacific, Atlantic, Indian, and Arctic Oceans.

Method of organization: _____

Transitions

Expressions like *next, for example*, and *in back of* are called **transitions.** Transitions are signals that show the connection between one idea and the next. They are important because they guide the reader through a paragraph and make it easy to understand. In this chapter you will learn some transitions for time relationships, spatial relationships, listing additional ideas, and giving examples. In later chapters you will learn other kinds of transitions.

Transition Signals That Indicate Time Relationships

after	eventually (Finally)	next
as	ever since	recently
as soon as	every year	since
at last	finally	soon afterward
at this point	first	the next day
before	from then on	(week, month, year)
by the time	in between	then
during	later	today
earlier	meanwhile	while

Transition Signals That Indicate Spatial Relationships

above	beside	near
across	between	next to
at the center	in back of	to the left
behind	in front of	to the right
below		

Transition Signals That List Additional Ideas

also	furthermore	next
another reason	in addition	one reason
besides	last	second
finally	last but not least	the most important reason
first	moreover	the third reason
first of all	most importantly	

Transition Signals That Give Examples

as an illustration	for instance	such as
especially	specifically	to illustrate
for example	(obviously)	

Identifying Transitions

A. Underline the transitions in the following paragraph.

English is only one of the world's 6,800 languages, but it is rapidly becoming a truly international language. First of all, English is the native language of over 400 million people scattered across every continent. In fact, English is used in some way by one out of seven human beings around the globe, making it the most widely spoken language in history. Approximately 50 percent of the world's books are published in English. In addition, three-quarters of all mail, faxes, and electronic messages are written in English. English is also the main language of science, technology, and international business. More than half of all scientific and technical journals are written in English, and over 80 percent of the information stored in computers around the world is in English. Over half of all business deals in Europe are conducted in English, and many more are negotiated in English in other parts of the international business community. Finally, English is the language of sports and entertainment. For example, it is the official language of both the Olympics and the Miss Universe Pageant. English is the language of over 60 percent of the world's radio and TV programs. More than ever before, English is now the most widely used and studied language of the world.

B. Look back at the three paragraphs on pages 35 and 36 and answer the following questions.

1. What kind of transitions were used in the paragraph describing the classroom?

_____

2. What kind of transitions did the author use to discuss the navigational cues of homing pigeons?

_____

3. What kind of transitions were used to explain the formation of oceans?

_____

Practicing Organization and Transitions

A. Think about the steps involved in planning a weekend trip to another city. Make a list of the steps and arrange them in time order.

Steps

- _____
- _____
- _____
- _____
- _____

Write a paragraph based on your list. Use transitions to connect your ideas.

_____
_____
_____
_____
_____
_____
_____
_____
_____
_____

READY TO WRITE

B. What could someone learn about you from looking at your bedroom? Make a list of the items you want to describe and their placement in the room. Arrange your list according to spatial order.

Items

- _____
- _____
- _____
- _____
- _____

(handwritten notes in margin: - facts, - feeling, - room partners, - smith)

Using spatial order, write a paragraph describing how your bedroom reflects your personality. Use transitions to connect your ideas.

_____

_____

_____

_____

_____

_____

_____

_____

_____

C. If you could live in any time period (past, present, or future), which one would you pick? Choose one and make a list of your reasons. Arrange the list in order of importance. You can begin or end with your most important reason.

Reasons

- _____
- _____
- _____

Write a paragraph based on your list. Use transitions to connect your ideas.

_____

_____

_____

_____

_____

_____

_____

_____

_____

On Your Own

A. Choose one of the topics below to develop into a paragraph.

- Qualities of a good doctor

- Description of your flag

- Reasons you like (or do not like) modern art

- Reasons cigarette advertising should (or should not) be banned

- Ways to get good grades

- How to prepare your favorite salad, soup, or dessert

- Design of a baseball field, basketball court, tennis court, or soccer field

- Benefits of having a job that requires a lot of travel

B. Use one of the prewriting techniques you practiced in Chapter 1 to get you started: brainstorming, clustering, freewriting, or writing in a journal.

C. Organize the ideas you generated by preparing a simple outline.

D. Write a topic sentence for your paragraph that has a single focus.

E. On a separate piece of paper, draft the paragraph. Remember to develop each of your supporting points with specific details. Use transitions to help guide your reader from one idea to the next.

Chapter Highlights

Complete the following paragraphs by filling in the blanks. You do not have to use exact words from the chapter as long as the ideas are correct.

There are several things to remember about writing a good paragraph in English. A paragraph is a group of sentences about _a single topic_. The most important sentence in a paragraph is the _topic sentence_. This sentence _controls_ everything else that goes into your paragraph. All the other sentences _support the topic sentence_ by _the details_. The topic sentence should state the _topic_ and _focus_. You will always need to support your topic sentences with _details_. In addition to a clear topic sentence and adequate support, a good paragraph must also have a _single focus_ and _logical order_. A paragraph has a single focus if all the supporting details _relate_ to the topic. A paragraph also needs to be easy to understand. This means it should have a logical organization. Three basic ways to organize information in a paragraph are by _time order_, _spacial order_, and _order of importance_. A good paragraph also needs _transitions_ to connect ideas.

CHAPTER 3

Revising and Editing

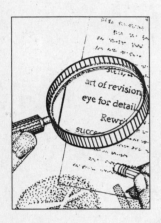

It has been said that there is no good writing, only good rewriting. Now that you have practiced the first two steps in the writing process, it is time to turn to the important step of revising and editing.

Step Three: Revising and Editing

REVISING

Don't forget that writing is a process. A very important part of that process is **revising.** The word *revision* is a combination of the root word *vision* and the prefix *re-* which means "again." When you revise, you "see again." That is, you look at your writing again to see how you can improve it. *Editing* is the final part of the revision step. What kind of changes should you make as you revise?

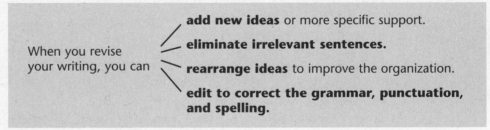

When you revise your writing, you can

add new ideas or more specific support.

eliminate irrelevant sentences.

rearrange ideas to improve the organization.

edit to correct the grammar, punctuation, and spelling.

Remember that it is almost impossible to write a perfect paragraph on your first try. You will need to read over your first draft to look for ways to improve it. First of all, check to see if there is a clear topic sentence. If not, you need to add one. Then, make sure all the sentences relate to the topic stated in the topic sentence. If you find a sentence that does not relate to the topic, delete it. As you read, check the organization. Ask yourself if the sentences are arranged in a logical order. If they are not, you need to rearrange them. Have you included transitional expressions? If not, add them. Also, make sure you have supported the topic with specific evidence such as details, facts, examples, and reasons. Finally, edit to check the grammar, punctuation, and spelling, and correct any mistakes you find.

Revising Checklist for Paragraphs

1. Is there a clear topic sentence? _____ yes _____ not yet

2. Do all the sentences support the topic sentence? _____ yes _____ not yet

3. Is there enough information to support the topic? _____ yes _____ not yet

4. Are the sentences organized in a logical order? _____ yes _____ not yet

5. Are there transition words to guide the reader from one idea to the next? _____ yes _____ not yet

If the answer to any of the questions is "not yet," you need to revise the paragraph.

Practicing Paragraph Revision

Read the following paragraphs and identify the problem, or problems, in each one. Use the Revising Checklist above to help you.

1. Ever since I got a part-time job after school, I've had trouble managing my time. By the time I get home from work, I don't have much time to do my schoolwork. I have to rush through my homework, and my assignments are always late. My social life is also suffering. I never seem to have enough time to be with my friends because I'm too busy working. Some of my friends have even stopped inviting me to go out with them. Worst of all, my demanding job leaves me little time for myself. I don't have time to do the things I really enjoy like reading magazines, taking pictures, and watching movies. Since I have so little time for studying, my grades are falling. Although I need the extra money I make, my job is really eating into my time.

    Problem: _____

2. My roommate and I are not very compatible. For one thing, we have different sleeping habits. He likes to stay up late watching TV or listening to music, but I prefer to go to bed early. In addition, he is a very neat person. He likes the room neat and clean at all times. On the other hand, I am very messy. I never hang up my clothes, and I always have books and papers scattered all over the room. Finally, while my roommate is a very social person, I am quite private. He likes to have his friends in our room and wants our room to be the party place. Luckily, we both like the same kind of music. On the other hand, I need my privacy and think of my room as my own quite space where I can be by myself.

    Problem: _____

3. First of all, it is easy to spend more money than I have when I use credit cards. I often charge so much that I can't afford to pay the whole bill when it arrives. Since I can only pay a small amount each month, it's going to take me years to pay off the balance. Another problem I have with credit cards is that it's too easy to buy on impulse. I often end up purchasing things I don't really need or even like that much. I love the new pair of shoes I just charged.

The interest rate on many of my cards is very high, and that's also upsetting. Some of my credit cards have a 19 percent interest rate, and the interest charges really add up! Unfortunately, I have ended up with a big debt very quickly. Therefore, I've decided to cut up my credit cards and never use them again.

Problem: _____

EDITING

After you revise your paragraph for content and organization, all you need to do is edit it. **Editing** means looking for and correcting mistakes in grammar, spelling, and punctuation. Finding the mistakes in your paragraph is not always easy, especially if English is not your native language. However, some mistakes are very common, so you should look for them first. The activities below will help you learn to correct some of the most common mistakes that students make.

Agreement of Subjects and Verbs

You already know that every English sentence must have a subject and a verb. In order for a sentence to be grammatically correct, the subject and verb must agree with each other. This means that if the subject is singular, the verb must be singular. If the subject is plural, the verb must be plural.

Example

> My friend was late for class.
>
> My friends were late for class.

For subject/verb agreement:

1. Find the main verb in each sentence.

2. Match the verb to its subject.

3. Make sure that the subject and verb agree in number.

Keep the following rules in mind:

- If subjects are joined by *and*, they are considered plural. Use a plural verb.

> My friend and I *were* late for class.

- If subjects are joined by *or* or *nor*, the verb should agree with the closer subject.

Use a singular verb if the subject closer to the verb is singular:

> Either Jason or Pat *drives* me to school.
> Neither Emily nor Ann *plans* to join the tennis club.

Use a plural verb if the subject closer to the verb is plural:

> Neither Ann nor her sisters *plan* to join the tennis club.

In the first sentence, *Ann* is closer to the verb. Because *Ann* is singular, the verb must be singular. In the second sentence, *her sisters* is closer to the verb, so the verb must be plural.

- Make the verb agree with its subject, not with the words that come between the subject and verb:

    This new **book** of poems **is** by Pablo Neruda.
    The **poems** in this book **are** by Pablo Neruda.

  The subject of the first sentence is *book*, which is singular. The subject of the second sentence is *poems*, which is plural.

- Use a singular verb with these pronouns:

anybody	everybody	somebody	nobody
anyone	everyone	someone	no one
anything	everything	something	none
either	one	neither	nothing

    Each of the students **is** required to write a five-paragraph essay. (*Each* is the subject.)
    One of the kids **wants** to take a nap. (*One* is the subject.)
    Everybody **wants** to start the movie now.

- Use a plural verb with these pronouns:

  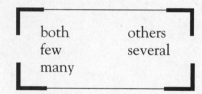

both	others
few	several
many	

    Several of the students **are** required to write a five-paragraph essay. (*Several* is the subject.)
    Others **want** to start the movie later.

- Use a singular verb with expressions of time, money, measurement, weight, and fractions:

    Twenty-five dollars **seems** like a reasonable price for this sweater.
    Twelve inches **equals** one foot.
    Three-fourths is more than one-half.

Practicing Agreement of Subjects and Verbs

Circle the correct verb for each of the following sentences.

1. One of my friends (has / have) a new car.

2. Everyone who works hard in this class (do / does) well.

3. Many of my friends (like / likes) the professor.

4. The instructor (don't / doesn't) give a lot of homework.

5. One of the reasons that I chose to go into medicine (is / are) that I like to work with people.

6. Fifty dollars (is / are) too much to spend on dinner at this restaurant.

7. Both Jane and her cousin (go / goes) to the University of Michigan.

8. The book and the movie (has / have) the same ending.

Agreement of Pronouns and Nouns

Remember that a pronoun must refer back to a specific noun. You must use the correct pronoun so your reader knows which noun your pronoun is referring to. A pronoun should agree in number with the noun it refers to. If a pronoun refers to a singular noun, you must use a singular pronoun. If a pronoun refers to a plural noun, you must use a plural pronoun.

> When a student eats in the cafeteria, he/she must show a student ID.
> When students eat in the cafeteria, they must show a student ID.

For pronoun/noun agreement:

1. Read over your paper, stopping at each pronoun. (Pay special attention to the pronouns *it*, *this*, *they*, and *them*.)

2. Identify the noun that the pronoun replaces. If you can't find the noun, you must add one or change the pronoun to a noun. If you find a noun, make sure it agrees with the pronoun.

As you saw earlier, the following pronouns are singular. Use a singular pronoun when you refer to them.

anybody	everybody	somebody	nobody
anyone	everyone	someone	no one
anything	everything	something	none
either	one	neither	nothing

Practicing Agreement of Pronouns and Nouns

Circle the correct verb for each of the following sentences.

1. Everyone on the team (comes / come) to practice every day.

2. All the team members (has / have) to work hard.

3. Each one of you students (is / are) improving.

4. He said, "Nobody (cares / care) about the game."

5. Someone (is / are) going to pay for this mistake.

Agreement of Possessives and Nouns or Pronouns

Pay special attention to possessives. Just as a pronoun and the noun it refers to must agree, a possessive must agree with the word it refers to. If the word referred to is singular, the possessive adjective or pronoun must be singular. If the word is plural, the possessive adjective or pronoun must be plural.

> The little **boy** is holding **his** mother's hand.
> The **children** are holding **their** mother's hands.
> **Each** of the girls had **her** own bedroom in the apartment.
> **Both** of our daughters have **their** own cars.
> Give it to **Jane.** It's **hers.**
> That **book** belongs to me. It's **mine.**

Practicing Agreement of Possessives and Nouns or Pronouns

Circle the correct possessive in each of the following sentences.

1. Both of the students forgot (his / their) notebooks.
2. Neither of my sisters owns (her / their) own house.
3. Matthew likes (his / their) meat cooked well done.
4. The Wexlers send (his / their) children to private school.
5. One of the women has retired from (her / their) job.
6. This isn't Connie's jacket. It's (my / mine).

Sentence Fragments

Every English sentence must have a subject and a verb. It must also express a complete thought. A complete sentence can stand alone. That is, it makes sense by itself. If a sentence lacks either a subject or a verb or is not a complete thought, it is called a **sentence fragment**.

There are three main kinds of fragments:

1. No Subject

    Fragment: Did very well on her math exam.

    Complete Sentence: Georgette did very well on her math exam.

2. No Verb

    Fragment: Both Alexander and his younger sister Lisa.

    Complete Sentence: Both Alexander and his younger sister Lisa enjoy tennis.

3. No Independent Clause/Incomplete Thought

    Fragment: Before I went to college.

    Complete Sentence: Before I went to college, I worked part time at a bank.

A dependent clause is often confused with a complete sentence because it contains a subject and a verb. However, it is not a complete thought. A dependent clause must be attached to an independent clause to form a complete sentence with a complete thought. Following is a list of the common words that are used to begin dependent clauses:

after	even though	unless	wherever
although	if	until	which
as	in spite of	whatever	while
because	since	when	who
before	so that	whenever	whom
despite	that	where	whose
even if	though	whereas	

Read the following example:

> Because the meteorologist predicted rain.

Although this clause has a subject and verb, it is not a complete sentence. It does not make sense by itself.

There are two possible ways to correct this mistake:

1. Make the dependent clause a complete sentence by removing the word *Because*.

   Sentence fragment: Because the meteorologist predicted rain.

   Complete sentence: The meteorologist predicted rain.

2. Attach the dependent clause to an independent clause.

   Sentence fragment: Because the meteorologist predicted rain.

   Complete sentence: Because the meteorologist predicted rain, I took my umbrella with me.

Correcting Sentence Fragments

A. Write *C* in front of each *complete sentence*. Write *F* in front of each *sentence fragment*. Then rewrite the fragments so that they are complete sentences.

Example:

__F__ Works out in the gym every day.

My father works out in the gym every day.

____ 1. I love visiting Monet's gardens in Giverny because gardening is my hobby.

_____

____ 2. Hockey a very dangerous sport if you don't have the right equipment.

_____

____ 3. Because I couldn't understand the homework,

_____ I was blamed by my ~~teacher~~ Teacher _____

____ 4. And ran out of gas on the way to work.

_____ I met shower rain and _____

____ 5. Whenever my next-door neighbor has time. we go playing soccer.

_____

_F_ 6. Although she had a bad cold, and hadn't slept well for days. ✓

_F_ 7. That my friend told me was the best movie he had ever seen.

B. Write a sentence using each of the following words.

1. after

   After I finish my homework, I took a shower.

2. although

   Although I went to Wal-Mart, I didn't buy anything

3. because

   I brought an umbrella because the sky looked gloomy.

4. before

   Before I go shopping, I checked the fridge.

5. if

   If I go to Canada, I will go to Yellowknife to see Aurora.

6. since

   I haven't been abroad since I was born in Japan. _good_

7. unless

   Unless you miss the last bus, you can come back to home

8. when

   When I get up at 5, the sun shine was intensely amazing.

9. until

   we need to say here

   I need to stay my room until my friend call me.

10. despite

   Despite losing a competition, I didn't feel bad.

Exchange sentences with a classmate. Check your partner's sentences. Are they all complete sentences?

Run-on Sentences

A **run-on sentence** occurs when two complete sentences are written as one sentence.

Example:

Sue loves to cook she is always in the kitchen.

There are three ways to correct this problem:

1. Use punctuation, usually a period, to separate the two sentences.

   Run-on sentence: Sue loves to cook she is always in the kitchen.

   Correct sentences: Sue loves to cook. She is always in the kitchen.

2. Use a coordinating conjunction (*and, but, for, so, or, nor, yet*) to connect the two clauses.

   Run-on sentence: The movie was boring we watched it anyway.

   Correct sentence: The movie was boring, but we watched it anyway.

3. Use a subordinating conjunction to connect the two clauses.

   Run-on sentence: I'm very hungry I didn't eat breakfast.

   Correct sentence: I'm very hungry because I didn't eat breakfast.

Correcting Run-on Sentences

Write *C* in front of each *complete sentence.* Write *R* in front of each *run-on sentence.* Then correct the run-on sentences.

_____ 1. I like my dentist he is very gentle.

_____

_____ 2. My son bought two T-shirts he thought they were so cool.

_____

_____ 3. It was too cold yesterday to ski we stayed in the lodge all day.

_____

_____ 4. When Jerry finishes work, he'll join us at the party.

_____

_____ 5. The Pilgrims first came to Plymouth, Massachusetts, in 1620 they were seeking religious freedom.

_____

_____ 6. If all twenty-five of us agree, it will be a miracle.

_____

_F_   7. Dennis called to say that his computer is making strange noises. ~~he~~ **He** thinks it is broken.

_____

_F_   8. They wanted to play golf, but we thought it was too hot we all went swimming instead.

_____

_F_   9. There are several ways to get from New York to Philadelphia, ~~the~~ **The** most convenient is by train.

_____

_____   10. I have a very good memory my husband, on the other hand, does not.

_____

Punctuation

Punctuation marks, such as commas, periods, and quotation marks, help readers interpret sentences. They determine how a sentence should be read and understood. Like most languages, English has certain rules of punctuation. The guidelines below will help you master some of the most important ones.

Period

- Use a period at the end of a statement:

    Argentina's economy is a mix of agriculture and industry.

- Use a period with most abbreviations:

Mr.	A.M.
Mrs.	P.M.
apt.	assoc.
Inc.	

Question Mark

- Use a question mark at the end of a question:

    Who is going to drive me to the airport?

Comma

- Use a comma to separate words or phrases in a series:

    The sea around Antarctica is home to dolphins, porpoises, whales, seals, and other sea creatures.

- Use a comma to separate independent clauses joined by a coordinating conjunction:

    We left in plenty of time, but we still missed the bus.
    I worked hard all day, so I went to bed early.

- Use a comma after many introductory phrases or clauses:

    Working late into the night, I drank several cups of strong coffee.
    Because I was tired, I went to sleep early last night.

- Use a comma before a direct quote:

    Christina said, "The train leaves in half an hour."

- Use a comma between the day of the month and the year:

    August 15, 1983

- Use a comma to separate cities from states:

    Billings, Montana
    Tallahassee, Florida

Colon

- Use a colon to introduce a series:

    The museum offers daily tours of the following collections: American, Asian, Classical, and European.

- Use a colon to introduce a long or formal quotation:

    Writing about his life, British philosopher Bertrand Russell said: "Three passions, simple but overwhelmingly strong, have governed my life: the longing for love, the search for knowledge, and the unbearable pity for the suffering of mankind."

Note: The first colon is used to introduce the quotation; the second one introduces a series.

- Use a colon to separate hours from minutes:

    3:15
    6:45

- Use a colon after the salutation in a formal letter:

    Dear Dr. Brody:
    Dear Ms. Rosen:

Quotation Marks

- Use quotation marks to enclose a direct quote:

    Jorge said, "I have already finished my homework."

- Use quotation marks to identify titles of songs, short stories, poems, articles, essays, and chapters from a book. Underline the titles of longer works such as books and newspapers. Underline the titles of paintings and other works of art. (If you are using a computer, the titles of longer works and art should be in italic type.)

    My favorite song is "Imagine" by John Lennon.
    One of Andrew Wyeth's best-known paintings is called <u>Christina's World.</u>

Practicing Punctuation

Punctuate the following sentences.

1. He was born in Portland on April 22, 1981
2. How many books have you read lately
3. We will have to leave by 530 PM
4. Dr. Anderson has a very full schedule today
5. I just finished reading Hemingway's novel The Old Man and the Sea
6. Most people like chocolate, but Jane is allergic to it
7. The restaurant has three specialties: grilled steak, marinated chicken, and fried shrimp
8. In conclusion, Mario Vargas Llosa is one of the greatest writers of the twentieth century
9. Marion said I can't go with you because I have too much homework
10. I think that Pablo Neruda's poem If You Forget Me is the most beautiful poem I've ever read

Capitalization

The following rules summarize the main uses of capitalization in English. If you are not sure when to capitalize a word, you should use your dictionary as a reference.

- Capitalize the first word of a sentence:

    Fishing is an important industry in Peru.

- Capitalize names. Capitalize a title that precedes a name:

    Dr. Lourie
    Professor Cantor
    David

- Capitalize the names of racial and ethnic groups:

  African American
  Asian
  Caucasian

  Exception: Do not capitalize the words *black* or *white* when referring to racial groups.

- Capitalize the names of specific geographical locations including countries, states, cities, towns, rivers, streets, and mountains:

  Paris
  Juniper Avenue
  Mount Rushmore

- Capitalize the days of the week, months, and holidays:

  Tuesday
  September
  Christmas

- Capitalize the names of religions:

  Buddhism
  Christianity
  Islam

- Capitalize nationalities and languages:

  Japanese
  Arabic

- Capitalize all words in a title except articles, prepositions, and conjunctions, unless they are the first or the last word in the title:

  "Give Peace a Chance"
  Men in Black
  Ready to Write More

Practicing Capitalization

Capitalize each of the following sentences correctly.

1. my russian history teacher is very handsome.

2. have you read romeo and juliet in your english literature class yet?

3. i meet with my advisor every tuesday and thursday morning.

4. my sister, ruth, has just returned from a trip to istanbul and athens.

5. shopping is one of the most popular activities of visitors to new york city.

Punctuation and Capitalization Review

Add the correct capitalization and punctuation to the sentences that follow.

1. traffic is causing serious pollution in some cities such as athens mexico city and los angeles

2. when will professor klein be in his office

3. my favorite poem is fire and ice by robert frost

4. i'll meet you on tuesday afternoon at 430 in front of the library on liberty street

5. mrs baker is one of the most inspiring speakers i've ever heard

6. the earliest maps anyone knows of were made by babylonians and egyptians over 4,000 years ago

7. the himalayas are the world's highest mountains

8. maria asked what time does the movie casablanca start

9. in 1980 the wildlife biologist george shaller began researching the panda in its natural habitat

10. professor dickens is sick so his tuesday night class will be canceled

Conquer Confusing Words

Learn the differences in meaning for these commonly confused words:

Accept	Verb, to take willingly (I accept your apology.)
Except	Preposition, to exclude (I want all the books except the green one.)
Advice	Noun, suggestion or recommendation (Please take my advice.)
Advise	Verb, to show the way, to give advice (I advised her to study hard.)
Affect	Verb, to influence (Did that change affect your decision?)
Effect	Noun, a change that occurred as the result of something (I don't like the effect coffee has on me.)
By	Preposition, used to show location (Give me the book that's by the calendar.)
Buy	Verb, to purchase (I will buy you a present at the store.)
It's	Contraction of *it is* (It's time to go.)
Its	Possessive (The school changed its policy.)
Right	Adjective, correct or proper (I know I'm right about this.)
Write	Verb, to put words on paper (Write your name on this paper.)
Suppose	Verb, to think or guess (I suppose it's all right to lend him money.)
Be supposed to	Verb phrase, should (Are you supposed to drink that?)
Than	Conjunction, used to show comparison (My car is older than yours. / I would rather walk than drive.)
Then	Adverb, after that (He brushed his teeth, and then he went to bed.)
Their	Possessive (They love their new car.)
There	Adverb, shows location (Put the book over there.)
They're	Contraction of *they are* (They're late for class.)

To	Preposition, in the direction of (He went to the store.)
Too	Adverb, also or to a greater degree (I want to go too. / This tea is too hot to drink.)
Two	Adjective, the number 2 (I saw two movies yesterday.)
Use	Verb, to utilize (I use sugar in my coffee.)
Used	Verb, past tense of *use* (He used all the soap.)
Be used to	Verb phrase, be accustomed to (I am used to living in a big city.)
Used to	Verb phrase, habitual past (I used to smoke cigarettes, but I don't any more.)
Whose	Relative pronoun, shows possession or association, *of whom* or *of which* (Whose books are these? / The man whose car was stolen is very angry.)
Who's	Contraction of *who is* (Who's the boss?)
Your	Personal pronoun, belonging to you (Your dress is very pretty.)
You're	Contraction of *you are* (You're a very nice person.)

Correcting Words

Work with a partner to write a sentence for each of the commonly confused words on the list. Then exchange your papers with another group and read their sentences. Do you see any mistakes? Correct the sentences where you find mistakes.

Editing Checklist for Essays

1. Is the first sentence of each paragraph indented? _____ yes _____ not yet

2. Do your subjects and verbs agree? _____ yes _____ not yet

3. Do your nouns, pronouns, and possessives agree? _____ yes _____ not yet

4. Are all the sentences complete (no fragments)? _____ yes _____ not yet

5. Have you eliminated run-on sentences? _____ yes _____ not yet

6. Is the punctuation correct in all the sentences? _____ yes _____ not yet

7. Does the first word of each sentence begin with a capital letter? _____ yes _____ not yet

8. Are all your words spelled correctly? _____ yes _____ not yet

If the answer to any of the questions is "not yet," go back and try to improve your paragraph.

Writing and Revising an Article

You are going to write an article for the travel section of a newspaper. The focus of your article will be how to plan a trip that will be economical, educational, and fun.

Prewriting

It is often easier to write after you have talked about the subject with some other people. In small groups, discuss ways to make travel economical, educational, and fun. Write the ideas that your group discusses in the chart below.

ECONOMICAL	EDUCATIONAL	FUN

Now complete the following steps as you draft your article.

1. Group the items on the list that go together.

2. Cross out items that do not belong.

3. On a separate piece of paper, make a simple outline of your paragraph.

Writing

On a separate piece of paper, write the first draft of your article.

Revising and Editing

Ask a classmate to read the first draft of your article and to make suggestions about how to revise it. He/She should use the Revising Checklist on page 43 and the Editing Checklist on page 56 as guides. Make a final copy of your article and give it to your teacher.

READY TO WRITE

You Be the Editor

There are ten mistakes in the following paragraph. Find and correct them. Then copy the corrected paragraph on a separate piece of paper.

There are a lot of interesting things to see and do in new york city. It is home to over 150 world-class museums. Their are art museums, science museums, photography museums, natural history museums, and even a museum of seaport history. New York is known for their rich variety of theater, music, and dance. From the bright lights of Broadway and the respected stages at Lincoln Center and Carnegie Hall to the high kicks of the Rockettes at Radio City Music Hall and incredible jazz at intimate clubs, there is something for everyone. Many people go to New York. For the wonderful restaurants. There are thousands of restaurants to please every palate and wallet If you are looking for a place to shop. You will find everything you can imagine. With more than 10,000 shops filled with brand names and bargains from around the world, NYC are a shopper's paradise. as for me, people-watching is my favorite New York pastime.

Chapter Highlights

Complete the following paragraph by filling in the blanks. You do not have to use exact words from the chapter as long as the ideas are correct.

      The last step in the writing process is _____ and

_____. When you revise a piece of writing, you look to see how
    2.

you can _____ it. When you revise your writing, you can
        3.

_____, _____, and _____. First of
    4.   5.   6.

all, make sure there is a clear _____. Then check to see if all
           7.

the supporting sentences _____ to the topic. If you find a
           8.

sentence that does not relate to the topic, _____ it. As you
           9.

read, check the organization. Ask yourself if the sentences are arranged in a

_____. Be sure you have included _____ to guide
    10.   11.

the reader from one idea to the next. It is also important to revise your

writing so that you have supported the topic with specific evidence such as

_____, _____, _____, and
    12.   13.   14.

_____. Finally, when you edit your writing, you correct the
    15.

_____, _____, and _____.
    16.   17.   18.

CHAPTER 4

Writing Essays

Essay writing builds on many of the skills you have already mastered in learning to write a paragraph. Once you know how to write a paragraph, it is not much more difficult to write an essay; an essay is just longer. Simply stated, an essay is a group of paragraphs about a specific subject. Like a paragraph, an essay makes and supports one main point. However, the subject of an essay is too complex to be developed in a few sentences. Several paragraphs are needed to support fully the main point of an essay. A typical essay contains five paragraphs, but many other types of essays are longer or shorter, depending on their purpose. In this book, you will learn the formula for a five-paragraph essay.

 TIP Although many essays do not fit into the five-paragraph formula, most essays follow some pattern of organization. The formula is simply a plan to help you arrange your ideas into a systematic order. It has a recognizable beginning, middle, and end. If you know how to write a typical five-paragraph essay, you will always have something to fall back on.

Parts of an Essay

An essay has three main parts: an **introduction**, several **supporting paragraphs**, and a **conclusion**. The supporting paragraphs are also called the **body**. Each part has its own special purpose. The introduction provides some background information on the subject and states the main idea in a thesis statement. The supporting paragraphs explain and support the main idea. The conclusion summarizes the main points.

BASIC PLAN OF A TYPICAL FIVE-PARAGRAPH ESSAY

INTRODUCTION

INTRODUCTION
Background Information
Gets reader's attention using one or more of the
following:
    Anecdotes
    Quotations
    Questions
    Facts and statistics
Thesis Statement
States the subject and focus of the essay

BODY

1st SUPPORTING PARAGRAPH
    Topic Sentence: States first supporting point
        Provides supporting details, examples, facts
2nd SUPPORTING PARAGRAPH
    Topic Sentence: States second supporting point
        Provides details, examples, facts
3rd SUPPORTING PARAGRAPH
    Topic Sentence: States third supporting point
        Provides details, examples, facts

CONCLUSION

CONCLUSION
    Makes final comments by doing one or more
    of the following:
        Restating main points
        Asking a question
        Suggesting a solution
        Making a recommendation
        Making a prediction

Read the following five-paragraph essay that a student wrote about the impact of
Latin pop music on the United States. Notice that the first line of each new
paragraph is indented. After you have read the entire essay, label the parts on the
lines provided.

Latin Pop Music Hits the United States

Since the late 1990s, Latin music has exploded onto
the U.S. music scene like never before. There has been a
steady increase in the record sales of Latin music albums
and a remarkable growth in the number of radio stations
devoted to Latin music. Musical talents from the Spanish-
speaking world have broken the U.S. market wide open. In
the process, they have added a little Latin spice and given
American musicians some friendly competition. With sales
at the top of the charts and Latin music sensations
continuing to grow in popularity, Latin music is not just
another fad; it is here to stay. Every revolution has its

leaders, and the recent Latin invasion, as it has been called, certainly has a few pioneering rockers that have helped to set the stage for the Latin pop explosion. Singers such as Gloria Estefan, Ricky Martin, and Shakira have been particularly helpful in bringing Latin beats to U.S. sound waves.

Gloria Estefan was one of the first Latin American artists to successfully incorporate Latin beats and sound with American pop music to produce hit songs across the United States. With her group, The Miami Sound Machine, Estefan began incorporating Cuban sounds into her pop-inspired music early in the 1990s. She quickly gained recognition as a powerful Latin singer whose unique music won the hearts and ears of many American music lovers. Pioneering artists such as Gloria Estefan have paved the way for the Latin superstars who followed. They helped tune the American ear to Latin music and continue to play an integral role in the developing Latin pop scene.

One of the more recent Latin pop sensations, and quite possibly the most successful, is Puerto Rico native Ricky Martin. Martin's unforgettable performance at the 1999 Grammy awards made the singer one of the most famous pop icons of the late 1990s. Soon after his performance, Martin began grinding out such fiercely Latin-inspired hits as "Living La Vida Loca" and "Shake Your Bon-bon," which earned the singer worldwide respect and helped to secure his role as king of Latin pop music. In this respect, Ricky Martin set the stage for an unmistakable Latin pop sound that quickly dismissed any doubts about the future of Latin pop music all over the Americas.

The latest Latin sensation to arrive on the American pop scene is Colombian singer Shakira. Shakira's long-awaited American debut album, *Laundry Service*, introduced a unique combination of Latin sounds and American pop-rock that has captivated critics and secured her a spot in the American pop scene. Shakira's distinctive style and unmistakable voice have been wholeheartedly embraced by the U.S. public. Her first single, "Wherever Whenever" met great success. Shakira is sure to have no problem challenging the American music industry.

Clearly Latin music has had a growing effect on current pop trends. With Latin vocalists such as Gloria Estefan paving the way and others like Ricky Martin setting the stage for Latin pop music sensations such as Shakira, Latin pop will not be leaving the United States any time soon. In short, if the successes of the later artists are any indication, Latin pop music will continue to grow as a driving force in the American music industry of tomorrow.

THE INTRODUCTION

The introduction is the first paragraph of your essay. It should capture the reader's attention and create a desire to read the rest of the essay. The introduction should start with a general discussion of your subject and lead up to a specific statement of your main idea, or thesis.

The format of an introductory paragraph is different from the format of most other kinds of paragraphs. In introductory paragraphs, the main idea is usually stated in the *last* sentence. This sentence is called the **thesis statement**.

The function of the introduction is
- to **capture the reader's interest.**
- to **provide background information.**
- to **state the main idea of the essay in a thesis statement.**

There are no specific rules for writing an introduction, but there are several techniques.

 TIP Many introductions use one or a combination of the following techniques to provide background information and capture the reader's attention.

- **Move from general to specific**

  This type of introduction opens with a general statement on the subject that establishes its importance and then leads the reader to the more specific thesis statement.

- **Use an anecdote**

  Another way to write an introduction is to relate an interesting story that will interest the reader in the subject. Newspaper and magazine writers frequently use this technique to begin their articles.

- **Use a quotation**

  A quotation is an easy way to introduce your topic. You can quote an authority on your subject or use an interesting quotation from an article. You can also be more informal and use a proverb or favorite saying of a friend or relative.

- **Ask a question**

  Asking one or more questions at the beginning of an essay is a good way to engage readers in the topic right away. They will want to read on in order to find the answers to the questions.

- **Present facts and statistics**

  Presenting some interesting facts or statistics establishes credibility.

Analyzing Introductions

Reread the introduction for the Latin music essay on page 61. Notice that the author began with a general statement about Latin pop music and then moved to a more specific statement about it.

Read the following sample introductions. Then, in small groups, identify the technique or techniques used in each one. Remember that authors often use a combination of techniques to write an introduction.

fact.

Introduce what is karate shallowly,

↓

background

1.　　　Karate, which literally means "the art of empty hands," is the most widely practiced of all the martial arts. It is primarily a means of self-defense that uses the body as a weapon for striking, kicking, and blocking. Having originated in the ancient Orient, the art of karate is more than 1,000 years old. It developed first as a form of monastic training and later became a method of self-defense. During the seventeenth century, karate became highly developed as an art on the Japanese island of Okinawa. Over the years, this ancient art has gained much popularity, and today karate is practiced throughout the world. More than a method of combat, karate emphasizes self-discipline, positive attitude, and high moral purpose. *thesis statement.*

Technique(s): _____

_____

Story

2.　　　One student looks at his neighbor's exam paper and quickly copies the answers. Another student finds out the questions on a test before her class takes it and tells her friends. Still another student sneaks a sheet of paper with formulas written on it into the test room. What about you? Would you be tempted to cheat on an exam if you knew you wouldn't get caught? According to a recent national survey, 40 percent of American teenagers would cheat under that condition. What is causing this epidemic of cheating in our schools? Most students cheat on tests because they feel pressure to get into a good college, because they want to avoid the hours of studying they need in order to get high grades, or simply because they are not concerned with honesty.

Technique(s): _____

_____

3.   Homicides cause the deaths of more children in Washington, D.C., than any other single type of injury, including car accidents, house fires, or drowning. Unfortunately, this phenomenon is not exclusive to Washington. The overcrowded neighborhoods of many big American cities, such as Detroit, Dallas, St. Louis, Atlanta, and Miami, are all plagued with senseless violent crime. Types of violent crime range from arson and burglary to assault, rape, and murder. The solution to this growing problem is not to build more and bigger prisons, but rather to examine and deal with the causes: easy access to guns, drug use, and overwhelming poverty.

Technique(s): _____→   *transition*

_____

4.   Misty, a five-month-old German shepherd puppy, goes to the hospital twice a week, but not to see a veterinarian. At this Veteran's Administration hospital, Misty is helping doctors—not the other way around. In what may seem like a role reversal, animals like Misty are visiting the halls of human illness to relieve a type of pain doctors cannot treat. Their therapy is love, both giving it and helping others return it to them. Pets ranging from dogs to tropical fish are showing up as therapists in hospitals, nursing homes, prisons, and other institutions.

Source: *Cobblestone*

Technique(s): _____

_____

5.   It is often said that "Two heads are better than one." For the past two years, the job of secretary in my office has been shared very successfully by two people. This "job-sharing" arrangement has worked out quite well for all involved. All over the business world, the interest in flexible employment arrangements, like job-sharing, is growing. Employers are beginning to realize that there are many talented people out there who are looking for alternatives to traditional patterns of employment. In a job-sharing arrangement, a full-time job is shared by two people. As an executive in a multinational firm, I feel that job-sharing is one way that organizations can meet the growing diversity of employees' needs. Not only is job-sharing helpful to employees, it also offers several advantages to employers. With two people working together, tasks tend to be completed more quickly, a wider range of skills is brought to the job, and most importantly, production is increased.

Technique(s): _____

_____

Thesis Statements

The thesis statement tells the reader what the essay will be about and what points you will be making in your essay. Your thesis statement should state the subject of the essay, explain the point of view the essay will take, or describe the ideas about your topic that you determined in your outline.

After you have presented some general background information, you need to narrow your focus. This is done in the thesis statement. A thesis statement is similar to a topic sentence. Just as a topic sentence controls the information for a paragraph, a thesis statement controls the information for an entire essay.

A good thesis statement —— **identifies the subject** of the essay.
—— **states the purpose** of the essay.
—— **tells the focus of the subject.**

Analyzing Thesis Statements

A. Underline the thesis statement in "Latin Pop Music Hits the United States" on page 61 and answer the following questions.

1. Does the thesis statement identify the subject of the essay? _____

2. Does it introduce the aspects of the subject that the essay develops? What are they? _____

B. Now look back at the sample introductions on pages 64 and 65 and underline the thesis statement in each one. Write the five thesis statements on the lines below.

1. _____
   _____

2. _____
   _____

3. _____
   _____

4. _____
   _____

5. _____
   _____

C. Look through several newspapers and magazines for interesting articles. Cut out three examples of introduction paragraphs and bring them to class. In small groups, discuss what makes each paragraph effective or ineffective as an introduction. What techniques did the writers use?

THE SUPPORTING PARAGRAPHS (THE BODY)

The body of an essay consists of several supporting paragraphs that support the thesis. Each supporting paragraph develops one point about the subject. Each paragraph begins with a topic sentence that is supported with specific details, facts, and examples.

 TIP Each main idea that you wrote down in your outline will become one of the supporting paragraphs. If you had three or four supporting ideas, you will have three or four supporting paragraphs.

Analyzing Supporting Paragraphs

Look again at the essay "Latin Pop Music Hits the United States" on pages 61 and 62.

1. Write the thesis statement here.

_____

_____

_____

2. What is the topic of the first supporting paragraph?

_____

_____

3. What is the topic sentence of that paragraph? What is its main idea?

_____

_____

4. Does it develop the first point mentioned in the thesis statement?

_____

5. What specific details are used for support?

_____

6. What is the topic of the second paragraph?

_____

_____

7. Does the topic sentence of that paragraph state its main idea?

_____

8. What is the second point mentioned in the thesis statement?

_____

9. What specific details support it?

_____

10. What is the topic of the third supporting paragraph?

_____

_____

11. Does the topic sentence of that paragraph state its main idea?

_____

12. What is the third point mentioned in the thesis statement?

_____

13. What specific details support it?

_____

_____

THE CONCLUSION

The final paragraph of your essay is the conclusion. It is the last thing your readers will see, so you want to make it interesting.

The purpose of this last paragraph is to summarize, without using the same words, the main points you have made in your essay. Your concluding paragraph should also leave your reader agreeing, disagreeing, or at least thinking about your thesis. There are several ways you can accomplish this.

 TIP There are no specific rules for writing a conclusion, but there are several techniques you can use. Many conclusions use one or a combination of the following techniques to wrap up the essay.

- **Restate your main points**

  When you use this method of finishing your essay, you restate the main points you presented in your essay. Make sure that you do not repeat your exact words. Try to figure out a new way to say them.

- **Ask a question**

  When you ask a provocative question, it will keep the readers thinking about the topic.

- **Suggest a solution; make a recommendation or prediction**

  Depending on the topic of your essay, the conclusion might be a good place for you to suggest a solution to a problem that you have discussed, or to make a recommendation or a prediction.

Analyzing Conclusions

A. Read the following sample conclusions. In small groups, identify the technique or techniques used in each one.

1.   Although John Lennon is no longer with us, his music is still very much a part of people's lives. He was a remarkable individual who spoke in a language that everyone could relate to. During the turbulent 1960s and 1970s, his optimistic message of peace, love, and happiness emerged. Today, perhaps more than ever, people recall the themes of his songs and look to them for answers. In the years to come, I predict that Lennon's message will continue to inspire countless generations.

Technique(s): _____ *prediction* _____

_____

2.   In conclusion, although sleep research is a relatively new field, it is a topic arousing considerable interest. A decade ago, only a handful of sleep disorder centers existed; however, today there are more than seventy-five. Consequently, scientists are beginning to unlock the mysteries of what Shakespeare called the "chief nourisher in life's feast." Still, there are numerous chapters to be added to the bedtime story. And then problem sleepers will be able to rest easy.

Source: *Your Health and Fitness.*

Technique(s): _____ *recommentaition* _____

_____

3.   During his life, Peter gained a great deal of power and exerted much influence on the course of Russian history. In summary, although he was not always completely successful, he worked very hard to modernize and westernize Russia. Although his actions were not always popular, everything Peter did was in the best interest of his country. By the end of his life, Peter had made significant progress toward achieving his goal of transforming Russia. Therefore, in my opinion, he deserves the name Peter the Great.

Technique(s): ___*Say fact,*___ *restate the book fact* ___

_____

4.   Technological improvements by car manufacturers continue at a healthy pace, and it is no coincidence that today's generation of cars is the safest ever. Crash tests demonstrate that many of today's cars earn top ratings for safety. However, real-life use will always demonstrate what we already know: that cars are only as safe as the people driving them.

Technique(s): _____ *solution.* _____

_____

5.   When Larry Bird retired from basketball, the sport lost one of its brightest stars—not only for the pure skills he brought to the game, but more importantly for the inspiration that he brought to both players and fans. Because of his skills, his work ethic, his value system, and his deep understanding of team dynamics, he will always be known as "Larry Legend." Will there ever be another one as talented and as selfless as Larry?

Technique(s): _____question._____

_____

6.   As I have shown, low-income senior citizens make up approximately 30 percent of the elderly population. These people are among the most vulnerable members of society because they depend so heavily on government programs for food, shelter, and medical needs. They are the ones who will suffer most severely if the government cuts back on its social programs.

Technique(s): _____

_____

B. Look through several newspapers and magazines for interesting articles. Cut out three examples of concluding paragraphs and bring them to class. In small groups, discuss what makes each paragraph effective or ineffective as a conclusion. What techniques did the writers use?

Practicing the Writing Process for an Essay

You are going to write a five-paragraph essay about the pressures of being a student. You can decide who your audience is going to be.

Step 1: Prewriting

Remember that the hardest part of writing is often *getting started*. To generate some ideas, try *brainstorming, clustering, freewriting,* or *keeping a journal* about the subject: the pressures of being a student. Then look over what you have written and decide on a focus for your essay. For example, are you going to discuss the pressures of being a student in a foreign country or in your native country? Are you going to talk about the pressures of being a high school student, college student, and/or graduate student? Are you going to talk about economic, academic, social, or emotional pressures?

It is sometimes difficult to decide which supporting points to use in your essay. Even after you have done some prewriting, you may still need to do more thinking and planning to find a focus if your subject is broad. However, there are a number of common ways to divide a general subject into three parts that you can use for the supporting paragraphs. For example, if your general subject is *the effects of computers*, there are several possible ways you could divide it. You might think about *time* and describe the effects of computers in the past, present, and future. Or you might consider *people* and write about the effects on children, adults, and the elderly. Still another way would be to analyze the economic, educational, and social effects of computers on *society*.

The following chart provides additional suggestions for how to divide a broad subject.

Place	People
a. local b. national c. international	a. students b. workers c. retired people
a. home b. work c. school	a. family b. friends c. co-workers
a. land b. sea c. air	a. children b. adults c. the elderly
Time	**Society**
a. past b. present c. future	a. economic b. political c. social/educational/religious
a. childhood b. adulthood c. old age	a. business b. science c. the arts

A. For each of the following essay topics, think of three main points that you could develop into an essay. You may use ideas from the chart on page 71 or come up with ideas of your own.

Example:

Topic: The Effects of Pollution

> Main Points:
> a. _Land_
> b. _Water_
> c. _Air_

1. Topic: The Benefits of Learning English

> Main Points:
> a. _____
> b. _____
> c. _____

2. Topic: The Impact of an Earthquake

> Main Points:
> a. _____
> b. _____
> c. _____

3. Topic: The Role of the Media in Our Lives

> Main Points:
> a. _____
> b. _____
> c. _____

4. Topic: The Changing Role of Women

> Main Points:
> a. _____
> b. _____
> c. _____

5. Topic: The Causes of Illiteracy

> Main Points:
> a. _____
> b. _____
> c. _____

B. On a separate piece of paper, make a simple outline of the ideas you generated from prewriting about the pressures of being a student to help you organize your thoughts as you plan your essay. Use your outline as a guide, and refer to it while you are composing.

Step 2: Writing

After you have spent some time thinking about your topic and doing the necessary prewriting, you are ready for the next step in the writing process: writing your essay. Begin with the introduction.

Write an Introduction

On a separate piece of paper, write the introduction for a five-paragraph essay on *the pressures of being a student*. Follow these steps:

1. Decide what technique or techniques you want to use to introduce your subject. Would an anecdote be effective? What about a quotation or some facts and statistics?

2. Write a thesis statement.

3. Work with a partner. Read and discuss each other's introductions.

Write the Supporting Paragraphs

A. **Look at your outline. Write a topic sentence for each supporting paragraph on the lines below.**

Topic sentence for first supporting paragraph:

_____

_____

Topic sentence for second supporting paragraph:

_____

_____

Topic sentence for third supporting paragraph:

_____

_____

B. **On a separate piece of paper, write a first draft of the supporting paragraphs for your essay on *the pressures of being a student*. Follow the principles you learned in Chapter 2 for writing effective paragraphs. Use the topic sentences you just wrote for each of the three paragraphs and support them with details, facts, or examples.**

Writing a Conclusion

Transition Signals That Introduce a Summary or Conclusion

Note: These signals should be followed by a comma.

consequently	in short	thus
finally	in summary	to conclude
in brief	last of all	to summarize
in conclusion	therefore	

Reread the introduction and supporting paragraphs you wrote on *the pressures of being a student*. On a separate piece of paper, write the conclusion to this essay.

Putting Together the First Draft

On a separate piece of paper, put together the first draft of your entire essay on *the pressures of being a student.* Include the introduction, three supporting paragraphs, and the conclusion. Give your essay a title that gives readers a good idea of what the essay is about. Save your paper. Your next step will be to revise it.

Step 3: Revise and Edit Your Essay

Remember, writing is a process that involves revising. After you have written the first draft of your essay, you need to revise it. It is often helpful to put your draft away for at least a day before you begin to revise it. The first thing you need to do is reread the whole essay. Keep in mind that your essay is a group of related paragraphs about one main idea. It should have an introduction that gets the reader's attention and states the main idea in a thesis statement. It should also have several supporting paragraphs, each with a topic sentence that supports the main idea, and a conclusion that ties the whole essay together. As you read the draft, make sure that you have included all three parts of an essay.

You also need to make sure that your essay is well organized. Ask yourself if the ideas follow a logical sequence from paragraph to paragraph. If the order is confusing, move the paragraphs around so that your main points are organized logically; for example, in time order, spatial order, or order of importance.

In addition, you need to pay attention to individual sentences within paragraphs. Remember that each paragraph must develop one main supporting point stated in the topic sentence. If a sentence in a paragraph does not support the main idea of the paragraph, you should delete it, rewrite it, or move it to another paragraph in the essay.

Check that you have not left out any important points or relevant information that would help support your topic or prove your thesis. If so, you need to add a sentence or paragraph to improve your essay.

Finally, edit to check the grammar, punctuation, and spelling, and correct any mistakes you find.

Practicing Revision

A. Reread the draft of the essay you wrote on *the pressures of being a student.* Answer the following questions.

1. What is the subject of your essay?

   _____

2. What is the purpose of this essay?

   _____

3. Who is your audience?

   _____

B. Revise your essay by answering each of the following questions.

Revising Checklist for Essays

1. Does the title of the essay give readers a good idea of what the essay is about? _____ yes _____ not yet

2. Does the introduction create interest in the topic for readers? _____ yes _____ not yet

3. Does the introduction state the main idea and the focus of the essay in a clear thesis statement? _____ yes _____ not yet

4. Does the first (second, third) supporting paragraph have a topic sentence that clearly states the first (second, third) main supporting point? _____ yes _____ not yet

5. Does every sentence in that paragraph support the topic sentence? _____ yes _____ not yet

6. Have irrelevant sentences been eliminated so that the paragraph has a single focus? _____ yes _____ not yet

7. Are the sentences in the paragraph arranged in a logical order? _____ yes _____ not yet

8. Are there transitions in the paragraph to guide the reader from one idea to the next? _____ yes _____ not yet

9. Do the supporting paragraphs provide adequate support and enough specific information to develop and prove the thesis of the essay? _____ yes _____ not yet

10. Are the supporting paragraphs arranged in a logical order? _____ yes _____ not yet

11. Does the conclusion summarize the main ideas of the essay? _____ yes _____ not yet

If the answer to any of the questions is "not yet," go back and try to improve your essay.

C. Peer Revising. Sometimes it is helpful to have someone else read your paper and offer suggestions on ways to improve it. Exchange drafts with a classmate and read each other's essay. Use the following worksheet as a guide for suggesting improvements in your partner's essay.

Writer: _____   Peer Editor: _____

1. What are the strengths of the essay? _____

   _____

   _____

2. What did you like best about it? _____

   _____

   _____

3. What weaknesses did you notice? _____

   _____

   _____

4. What suggestions for improvement can you offer? _____

   _____

   _____

Incorporate any suggestions your partner has made that you agree with.

D. Use the checklist on page 75 to edit your essay. Correct all the grammar, punctuation, capitalization, and spelling errors before you copy it over or type it.

On Your Own

Choose one of the other topics on page 72 and write a five-paragraph essay. Be sure that your essay includes an introduction, a body, and a conclusion.

Chapter Highlights: Crossword Puzzle

ACROSS

2. One way to get your reader's attention is to ask a _____.
4. Paragraphs of an essay that develop and support the thesis
6. A short, interesting, or amusing story about a person or an event
7. To describe something that will happen in the future
8. States the main idea of the essay and is often the last sentence in the introduction
10. Paragraph of an essay that captures the reader's interest and states the thesis
12. One technique authors use in their conclusion is to make a _____ about the future.
13. To give advice or suggest
16. To restate the main points, using new words
17. Transition words and phrases add _____ to a paragraph and essay.

DOWN

1. The name of an essay is the _____.
2. A _____ is sometimes used at the beginning of an introductory paragraph.
3. A group of sentences about one main topic
4. An introduction gives _____ information to capture the reader's attention.
5. Paragraph of an essay that summarizes the main points
8. Sentence in a paragraph that states the main idea
9. Presenting facts and _____ about a subject helps establish credibility.
11. Another word for *subject* is _____.
14. A group of paragraphs about one subject
15. Your first attempt at writing on a topic

PART 2

TYPES OF ESSAYS

Now that you have learned the basic structure of an essay, you will practice writing different types of essays. There are many different kinds of essays. Sometimes your teacher will decide which type of essay you must write. But other times it may be up to you to choose a type of essay that fits your purpose.

Following are some of the basic types of essays and their purposes:

ESSAY TYPE	PURPOSE
Process	to describe the sequence of steps in a procedure
Division and Classification	to describe the logical divisions of a topic or the parts of an object
Causes and Effects	to analyze the causes or effects of a situation
Comparison/Contrast	to show the qualities that are similar or different between two things
Problem/Solution	to describe a problem and evaluate possible solutions

Work with a Partner

With a classmate, discuss which type of essay you would write for each of the following purposes.

- To analyze why a recent presidential campaign was unsuccessful

- To discuss the reasons you chose your current major

- To suggest ways to solve the problem of high unemployment in your country

- To explain how to install a program on your computer

- To describe the types of friends you have

- To evaluate the differences between two treatments for back pain

- To teach your co-workers how to use a new copy machine

- To describe the categories of movie ratings

The chapters in Part 2 will give you practice in writing some of the basic types of essays. In this way, you will learn how using these patterns can help you organize your ideas.

CHAPTER 5

Process

When your purpose in writing is to inform your readers about how to do something or to describe the order of steps in a procedure, you will write a **process essay**. For instance, when you explain procedures such as how to train a dog to do tricks, how to give a good haircut, or how to study for a math test, you are describing steps in a process.

 TIP When you organize the steps in a process, you should arrange them according to time order.

In academic writing, the process essay is especially important in scientific and technical fields. For example, it is used to describe biological processes such as cell division, chemical processes such as photosynthesis, and technical processes such as how a diesel engine works.

The Language of Process: Useful Phrases and Sentence Patterns

Transition Signals That Indicate the Order of Steps in a Process

first	soon afterward	every time
the first step	the third step	whenever
from then on	then	meanwhile
next	at this point	while
the next step	as	during
before	as soon as	the last step
after	when	finally
after that		

The following sentence patterns are useful in writing thesis statements for process essays:

1. **It is** | easy
simple
not difficult | **to** _____ **if you have the right** | tools.
equipment.
materials.
ingredients.

It is easy to change a flat tire if you have the right equipment.

2. _____ **is easy when you follow** | these steps.
these directions.
these instructions.
this procedure.

Making a delicious omelet is easy when you follow these steps.

3. **There are** | three
four
several | **major steps involved in** _____.

There are three major steps involved in studying for an exam.

Write a sample thesis statement for a process essay on each of the following essay topics. Use a variety of the sentence patterns modeled above.

Example

Topic: How to write an essay

Thesis statement: _Writing a good essay is easier if you follow three main steps._

1. Topic: How to impress your teacher or boss

   Thesis statement: _____

   _____

2. Topic: How to build bigger muscles

   Thesis statement: _____

   _____

3. Topic: How to make a pizza

   Thesis statement: _____

   _____

4. Topic: How to build a tree house

   Thesis statement: _____

   _____

5. Topic: The best way to lose weight

Thesis statement: _____

_____

6. Topic: How to make a beautiful flower arrangement

Thesis statement: _____

_____

DESCRIBING THE STEPS IN A PROCESS

You have just made a bookcase in a woodworking class. Now you need to write a one-paragraph description of the process for your teacher. Look at the ten step-by-step drawings below.

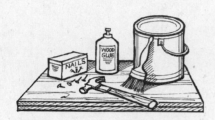

1. Assemble: wood, nails, glue, a hammer, a saw, sandpaper, and paint.

2. Cut: 2 side pieces $11^5/8$" by 28"
3 pieces for top, bottom, and shelf, $11^5/8$" by $13^1/2$"
1 back piece 15" by 28"
two 10" molding strips

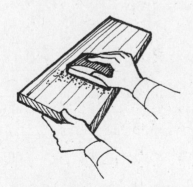

3. Sand each piece of wood.

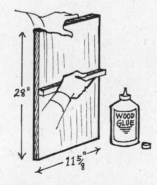

4. Glue one molding strip to each side piece, 14" down from top.

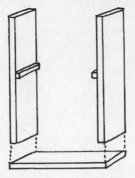

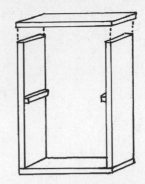

5. Nail side pieces to bottom.　　　6. Nail the top in place.

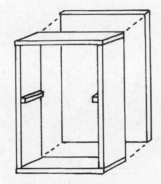

7. Nail the back piece in place.　　　8. Paint the bookcase and shelf.

9. Let dry 2 hours.　　　10. Slide the shelf into place.

Practicing the Description of a Process

On a separate piece of paper, write a one-paragraph description of the process. Use the drawings as a guide. Be sure to include a topic sentence that states your purpose and include transition signals to indicate the order of the steps.

WRITING A PROCESS PARAGRAPH

A. Read the following conversation between a student and a librarian.

STUDENT: Excuse me. I'm doing research for a paper I'm writing on the effects of global warming. Can you tell me how to find some current articles on this subject?

LIBRARIAN: Certainly. The best place to begin is over here in the reference section. Are you familiar with how to use the computerized card catalog?

STUDENT: Not really. I've only used it once, and I think I've forgotten how it works.

LIBRARIAN: It's really quite easy. All you need to do is type in your topic here and press the return key. The computer will search its database of magazines and journals and will give you a list of all the articles related to your topic. You can choose which ones you want to look up, and you can print out the list of citations.

STUDENT: OK. That seems fairly straightforward. But my professor said we could only use articles from the past three years.

LIBRARIAN: That's no problem. The dates of the articles are given right here, so you can just look up the most recent ones.

STUDENT: That's great. Is there anything else I need to know?

LIBRARIAN: Well, another good feature of this program is that it gives you a brief summary of the main points of the article.

STUDENT: How can I look at that?

LIBRARIAN: Just click on the box that says *abstract*. Here, I'll show you.

STUDENT: This sure beats looking through piles of magazines for the right information. Thank you so much for helping me.

LIBRARIAN: You're welcome. If you have any more questions, I'll be at the reference desk.

STUDENT: Oh, one more thing before you go. Where are the magazines and journals?

LIBRARIAN: They're in the periodical section on the second floor. You can't take them out, but there are several copy machines in that area if you need to make a copy of any of the articles.

STUDENT: Thanks again.

B. Using information from the conversation, write a paragraph about how to use a computerized index to do research. Write your paragraph on a separate piece of paper.

"Wow! How long did it take you to train him to do that?"

Read the essay "How to Train Your Pet."

How to Train Your Pet

Have you ever wondered how the animals you see on TV and in movies are trained to perform such amazing tricks? Many of their trainers use a technique based on the teaching methods developed by behavioral psychologists such as B. F. Skinner. Skinner studied techniques for reinforcing desired behaviors in animals. Animals can be taught many sophisticated tricks using Skinner's techniques. If you want to teach your pet to do a trick, you must understand the technique psychologists call "shaping." Shaping means reinforcing, or strengthening, behaviors that you want to encourage. Here is how you can apply his techniques to training your pet to do tricks.

Begin by making some decisions. First of all, you need to choose your subject. You can pick any household pet, such as a cat, hamster, parrot, or dog. Suppose, for example, that you want to teach your dog to do a trick. The next thing to do is to choose a reward. Food is usually the easiest reward to use. Keep in mind that in order for food to be an effective reward, your dog has to be hungry. Don't try to teach him a new trick right after he has eaten a big meal. Also, a reward is most effective when it is given at the same time that the dog performs the desired trick. Since you will not always be able to give the dog food as quickly as you would like to, you will need to develop a "conditioned reinforcer." You can do this by connecting the food with something else, such as ringing a bell. In this case, the sound the bell makes is the conditioned reinforcer.

You are now ready to begin conditioning the dog to respond to the bell. Get out about 40 small dog biscuits. Toss a few of them to your dog, one at a time, at a rate of about one or two biscuits a minute. As soon as the dog begins eating the biscuits, ring the bell and then throw him another biscuit. Wait about thirty seconds and then repeat the steps. When you ring the bell, do not make any other sound or movement. Give the biscuit only when the dog is standing in the place where he gets his food. When your dog reaches the point where he goes to the food place whenever you ring the bell, you are ready to begin teaching him the trick.

At this point, you need to choose the trick you want to teach. An easy trick is teaching your dog to roll over. Shape the dog's behavior by reinforcing anything that resembles the behavior you are trying to teach. Begin by reinforcing any attempt to lie down. Then reinforce any movement of his body when he is lying down. Every time you reinforce any of his behaviors that resembles rolling over, immediately give him a biscuit and ring the bell. In this way, he will begin to associate the sound of the bell with the trick. Continue reinforcing closer approximations of rolling over with the biscuits and the bell. During the teaching session, do not touch the dog, talk to him, or in any way distract him. A normal dog, according to Skinner, will learn the trick within five minutes.

As you can see, it is really not very difficult to train your pet to do a trick. It is only a matter of a little time and some effort. Once you have established a conditioned reinforcer, you can easily teach your dog a new trick by shaping his behavior. However, if you want to teach your dog another trick, you must eliminate the first behavior by no longer reinforcing it. Eventually, he will stop rolling over and will be ready to learn something new.

Work with a Partner

Answer the following questions with a partner.

1. What technique does the author use to introduce the topic? (See Chapter 4.)
2. What process is the author describing?
3. How does the author organize the information?
4. Make a list of the steps in the process.

   a. _____

   b. _____

   c. _____

5. What transitions did the author use to connect the ideas in the essay? Underline them.
6. What audience do you think the author had in mind when he wrote this essay?

ESSAY PLAN: PROCESS

The guidelines below will help you remember what you need to do in each part of a process essay.

Introduction

1. State what the process is and why it is important.
2. Define the process.
3. State the purpose for explaining the process.
4. List any equipment, ingredients, or supplies needed to perform the process.
5. Write a thesis statement that states the focus of your essay.

Supporting Paragraphs

1. Describe the steps in the process, using time order.
2. If there are a lot of steps, group them into several main categories.

Conclusion

1. Review why the process is important.
2. Summarize the main steps in the process.

Writing a Process Essay

In this activity, you will practice writing an essay that describes the steps in a process. Follow these steps:

Prewriting

A. Choose one of the following topics and make a list of the steps in the process in the space below.

- How to wash a car
- How to study for an exam
- How to make rice, tea, coffee, noodles, a salad, etc.
- How to annoy your teacher, your boss, or your parents
- How to write a good paragraph or essay
- How to make a paper airplane, a clay pot, a knitted scarf, etc.
- Your own topic

READY TO WRITE

B. Organize your list according to time order in the space below. On a separate piece of paper, prepare an outline of your essay.

Writing

On a separate piece of paper, write the first draft of your essay. Use the essay plan on page 85 to help you draft your essay. Be sure to provide some background information about the process in the introduction and include a clear thesis statement of purpose. Describe the steps in the supporting paragraphs and organize them according to time order. End with a conclusion that summarizes the steps and restates the purpose.

Revising and Editing

A. Personal Revising. Wait at least one day, and then revise your essay using the checklist on page 75. Also, make sure that you have adequately described each step in the process. Write or type a revised version of your essay.

B. Peer Revising. Exchange drafts with a classmate. Use the following worksheet as a guide for suggesting improvements in your partner's essay.

Writer: _____ Peer Editor: _____

1. What are the strengths of the essay? _____

_____

_____

2. Did the introduction identify the process and
state why it is important?   _____ yes _____ no

3. What weaknesses, if any, did you notice in the organization? _____

_____

_____

4. What suggestions can you offer to improve the organization? _____

_____

_____

5. Did the author include enough transitions to guide
you from one step to the next?   _____ yes _____ no

6. Was each step in the process adequately explained?   _____ yes _____ no

7. Did the author include an effective conclusion?   _____ yes _____ no

If not, how can it be improved? _____

_____

_____

Incorporate any suggestions your partner has made that you agree with.

C. Editing. Use the checklist on page 56 to edit your essay. Correct all the grammar, punctuation, capitalization, and spelling errors before you copy it over or type it.

Explore the Web

You can use the Web to find instructions for how to do or make lots of things. Explore the Web to find out how to do something you are interested in such as juggling three balls, creating a Web site, planting a garden, baking bread, refinishing a piece of furniture, or making an origami crane. Use the information to write a process essay.

You Be the Editor

The following recipe is an example of a process paragraph. The content of the recipe is correct, but there are eight mistakes. Find the mistakes and correct them. Then copy the corrected paragraph on a separate piece of paper.

Recipe

If you like to eat or bake delicious cookies, you will love this recipe. Soften ½ pound of butter and mix it together with 2 cups off sugar. Stir in 3 beaten egg and 3 tablespoons of lemon juice. Then add 4 cups of flour 1 teaspoon of baking powder and 2½ teaspoons of nutmeg. As soon as the mixture is thoroughly combined, form the dough into a large ball and refrigerator it for at least 1 hour. When your ready to bake the cookies, divide the ball of dough in half. Roll the dough out so that is ⅛ inch thick. It will be easier if you use a rolling pin. Cut the cookies into shapes, using the open end of a glass or cookie cutters if you have them. Put the cookies on greased cookie sheets and bake them at 375 degrees for 6 minutes. To make them sweeter and more festive, frost them with colored frosting. With this recipe, the hardest part is trying not to eat to many!

On Your Own

Choose one of the following topics and write a process essay. Make sure that your introduction states the process and your purpose for explaining it. Remember to organize the steps of the process according to time order.

1. How to find a job
2. How to apply to a university in your country or the United States
3. How to make up with a friend after an argument
4. How to start a business
5. How to do a search on the Web
6. Your own topic

CHAPTER 6

Division and Classification

Classification is another way to organize a topic for an essay. A broad topic is often easier to write about when you divide it into individual parts and then classify the parts into groups that have something in common. In other words, you divide a topic into groups of things that share similar characteristics.

The prewriting (including planning) stage is a very important part of the process of writing a classification essay. Before you write, you need to spend time thinking about your topic and how you want to divide it into groups. Clustering is a good technique to use to help you identify your groups.

TIP   It is helpful to find at least three divisions to use. In other words, try to think of at least three separate groups. For example, if you were writing an essay on types of energy, you could divide them into three groups: wind, hydraulic, and solar. Make sure the groups do not overlap.

To write a classification essay, you should begin by dividing your topic into three (or more) complete and separate groups. The number of groups will equal the number of supporting paragraphs you have in your essay. For example, if you divide the topic of energy into three groups, you will have three supporting paragraphs. You will describe wind energy in one paragraph, hydraulic energy in the next paragraph, and solar energy in the third supporting paragraph. Remember to give examples of typical things in this group so the reader can see how each group is different from the others.

Classification is one of the most common ways to organize an essay in academic writing. In a business class, you might be asked to classify and discuss the various types of insurance policies. In a political science class, you might need to describe the three branches of the U.S. government. In a chemistry class, you might have to group types of chemical reactions.

The Language of Classification: Useful Sentence Patterns

The following sentence patterns are useful in writing topic sentences and thesis statements for classification paragraphs and essays:

1. **There are**
   | three | kinds |
   | two | types | **of** _____ .
   | four | classes |
   | several |

There are three kinds of energy: wind, hydraulic, and solar.

2. **I can**
   | divide | parts: |
   | classify | _____ **into three** | groups: _____ .
   | group | types: |
   | categorize | kinds: |

I can divide my computer games into three groups: action, simulation, and strategy.

3. _____ **can be**
   | divided | three parts: |
   | classified | **into** | two groups: _____ .
   | grouped | three types: |
   | categorized | several kinds: |

News articles can be divided into three types: local, national, and international.

Write a sample thesis statement for a classification essay on each of the following essay topics. Use a variety of the sentence patterns modeled above.

Example:

Topic: Restaurants in my city

Thesis statement: _The restaurants in my city can be divided into three groups:_ _fast-food restaurants, family-style restaurants, and gourmet restaurants._

1. Topic: Courses I have taken

   Thesis statement: _____

   _____

2. Topic: Successful people

   Thesis statement: _____

   _____

3. Topic: Friends I have had

   Thesis statement: _____

   _____

4. Topic: Automobile drivers

   Thesis statement: _____

   _____

5. Topic: Television shows

   Thesis statement: _____

   _____

6. Topic: Electronic devices

   Thesis statement: _____

   _____

DIVIDING A SUBJECT

There is often more than one way to divide a subject into groups. The important thing to remember is that you must choose one basis for dividing the topic. For example, the subject *cars* can be classified into groups by size: compact, intermediate, and full size. Cars can also be classified by manufacturer, price, or body style.

The way you divide your topic depends on the purpose of your essay. However, the groups you choose must be separate and distinct. In other words, the groups must not overlap. For example, if you were writing an essay on types of clothes, you might use the following groups: formal clothes, work clothes, and casual clothes. In this case, the basis for division would be where the clothes are worn. You could also classify clothes according to season and have four groups: spring clothes, summer clothes, fall clothes, and winter clothes. But you could not divide clothes into casual clothes, work clothes, and summer clothes because the groups overlap. A pair of shorts could be put in the casual clothes group and in the summer clothes group. Similarly, a linen suit fits in two of the groups: work clothes and summer clothes.

Practicing Classification

How many ways can you think of to divide the students in your class into groups? Make a list of several different ways. Identify the basis of division for each one and list the groups.

Example

Basis for Division: <u>Dominant hand</u>

Groups:

<u>right-handed</u>

<u>left-handed</u>

1. Basis for Division: _____

    Groups:

    _____   _____

    _____   _____

2. Basis for Division: _____

   Groups:

   _____   _____

   _____   _____

3. Basis for Division: _____

   Groups:

   _____   _____

   _____   _____

ANALYZING A CLASSIFICATION ESSAY

Remember that there are often several ways to divide a subject into groups. The way you divide your topic depends on the purpose of your essay. In the essay below, "A Guide to Food Groups," the purpose is to describe how the U.S. Department of Agriculture classifies groups of foods that make up a healthy diet.

Read the essay below.

A Guide to Food Groups

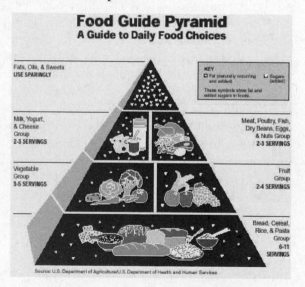

Everybody knows that the foods you eat affect your health. The nutrients in food keep your body healthy and help it grow. Without proper nutrition, your body and mind cannot function their best. Since no single food provides all the nutrients you need, eating a variety of foods increases your chances of getting all the vitamins, minerals, and other nutrients necessary for good health. To help people choose a healthy diet, the United States Department of Agriculture (USDA) created the Food Guide Pyramid in 1992. The pyramid shows the groups of foods that the USDA feels make up a healthy diet and how much of the foods should be eaten each day for the best health. The Food Guide Pyramid divides the foods we eat into six groups: the Grain Group, Vegetable Group, Fruit Group, Milk Group, Meat Group, and Fats Group.

The first group, the Grain Group, includes bread, cereal, rice, and pasta. This group is at the bottom of the pyramid because the USDA feels foods in this group should make up the biggest part of what you eat all day. That's because bread, cereal, rice, and pasta are all great sources of carbohydrates, which the body uses as its major source of energy. Foods in this group are usually low in fat and are the preferred fuel for our brain, nervous system, and muscles. The Food Guide Pyramid suggests that people eat six to eleven servings from this group each day. Some examples of what counts as one serving include 1 slice of bread, ½ cup of cooked rice or pasta, ½ cup of cooked cereal, 1 ounce of cold cereal, or ½ bagel or English muffin.

The next two food groups are the Vegetable Group and the Fruit Group. The foods in these groups come from plants. These two groups are toward the bottom of the pyramid because vegetables and fruits are an important part of a healthy diet. Vegetables and fruits provide many important vitamins and minerals. They also provide carbohydrates for energy, as well as lots of fiber to help your digestive system work properly. The Food Guide Pyramid suggests that people eat three to five servings from the Vegetable Group each day. A cup of raw vegetables, ½ cup of cooked vegetables, or ¾ cup of vegetable juice each count as one serving. The Fruit Group is also important for a healthy diet. The Food Guide Pyramid suggests two to four servings of fruits a day. One serving equals a medium apple, banana, or orange; ½ cup of chopped, cooked, or canned fruit; or ¾ cup of fruit juice.

The fourth and fifth food groups, the Milk Group and the Meat Group, are shown on the next level of the Food Guide Pyramid. The foods in these groups come mostly from animals. The Milk Group and the Meat Group are higher up on the pyramid because you don't need to eat as many of them in one day as you do of foods lower down on the pyramid. The Milk Group includes milk, yogurt, and cheese. Eating and drinking milk, yogurt, and cheese is the best way for you to get calcium, which is very important for strong teeth and bones. These foods also provide protein. Proteins build and repair body tissue, make hormones, and help fight infections. The Food Guide Pyramid suggests that people eat two to three servings from this group each day. Here are some examples of what counts as one serving: 1 cup of milk or yogurt or 1½ to 2 ounces of cheese. The Meat Group includes poultry, fish, dry beans, eggs, and nuts, as well as meat. These foods are important sources of protein, calcium, iron, and zinc. The Food Guide Pyramid suggests that people eat two to three servings from this group each day. One serving is 2 to 3 ounces of cooked lean meat, poultry, or fish; 1 egg, ½ cup of cooked dry beans, or 2 tablespoons of peanut butter.

The last group, the Fats Group, is represented at the small tip of the Pyramid. Foods such as salad dressings and oils, cream, butter, margarine, sugars, soft drinks, candies, and sweet desserts are in this group. These foods provide calories but not much nutrition. Most people should use them sparingly in their diet.

The Food Guide Pyramid is a tool that helps you choose what foods to eat in order to get all of the nutrients your body needs. The foods at the base should provide the biggest part of your diet. As you go up the pyramid, the requirements get smaller as the pyramid gets smaller. The Food Guide reminds us to eat a variety of foods because no single food provides all the nutrients you need.

Work with a Partner

A. Answer the following questions with a partner.

1. What is the thesis statement of the essay? *in end of the sentens*
2. What are the six main food groups? *each paragraph's top or thesis thesis statement*
3. What examples does the author use to describe each group? *Topic or end*
4. What signal words did the author use to organize the essay? Underline them in the essay.

B. Do some research.

1. This is not the only way to classify foods that make up a healthy diet. In fact, many people disagree with this method of classification. Do some research about other ways this topic can be classified. You can do a search on the Web to find some recent information. Type in the key words "food pyramid" and read some of the articles you find. Here is a site that you may find helpful: http://nutrition.tufts.edu/publications/matters/2001-10-01.html

2. Using the above essay as a model, write a classification essay about foods that make up a healthy diet that uses another method of classification. Refer to the essay plan below. Write your essay on a separate piece of paper.

3. Draw an illustration to go with your essay. Label the parts of your illustration.

ESSAY PLAN: CLASSIFICATION

The guidelines below will help you remember what you need to do in each part of a classification essay.

Introduction
1. Provide background information about the topic to be classified.
2. Explain the purpose for the classification.
3. Describe how you are going to divide the topic into groups.
4. State the number and names of the groups.
5. Provide a clear thesis statement.

Supporting Paragraphs
1. Identify and describe one group in each supporting paragraph.
2. Explain the common characteristics of the members of each group.
3. Give examples of items in each group.

Conclusion
1. Restate the method of classification.
2. Summarize the groups.

Completing a Classification Essay

You are a meteorologist. You have been asked to write an article describing the three main groups of clouds for your city's science museum. Here is the introductory paragraph that you have written for the article:

> The scientific study of clouds began in 1803 when Luke Howard, a British pharmacist and amateur meteorologist, introduced the first system for classifying clouds. Although many other procedures for cloud classification have been devised over the years, Howard's system is so simple and effective that it is still in use today. It is based on the shape, distribution, and altitude of clouds. He identified ten different categories, but they are all variations of three basic cloud forms. Howard used their Latin names to identify them: *cirrus* (meaning "curl"), *stratus* ("spreading out in layers or sheets"), and *cumulus* ("a pile or heap").

Now you need to write the three supporting paragraphs. Here are the pictures you will use as the basis for these three paragraphs. There is a lot of information, so you will have to decide which items you want to include.

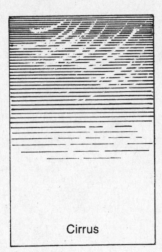

Cirrus

Stratus

Cumulus

Cirrus Clouds

—found about 5 miles (8 kilometers) above sea level
—highest of all clouds
—look white, curly, feathery, delicate, streaky, wispy, thin
—sometimes called "mares' tails" because they tend to look like the tails of horses
—move at speeds of 100 to 200 miles per hour (160 to 320 kilometers per hour), but their height makes their speed seem much slower
—made entirely of ice crystals because it is so cold at that altitude

Stratus Clouds

—found 1 to 4 miles (1.6 to 6 kilometers) above the Earth
—usually arranged in smooth, flat layers
—look like a gray sheet or blanket, but not very thick, so blue sky often shines through

—sometimes called "mackerel sky" in English because they look like the scales of a fish
—often signal that bad weather may be coming
—made of water droplets

Cumulus Clouds

—found about 1 to 4 miles (1.6 to 6 kilometers) high
—their tops may rise to great heights, making them look like rising towers
—detached, look like cauliflowers
—large masses of clouds, fluffy and dome-shaped with a flat, gray base
—usually seen in summer
—if they become too dense and vertical, they often produce heavy rain, lightning, and thunder
—sometimes called "thunderheads"
—tornadoes come from thunderheads
—made of water droplets

1. Draft your three supporting paragraphs on a separate piece of paper.

2. Exchange drafts with a classmate. Use the checklists on pages 56 and 75. Discuss any suggestions that your partner has for revision and editing. Include the introduction and add a short conclusion. Write or type a revised version of your essay.

Writing a Classification Essay

In this activity you will practice writing an essay that classifies a topic into several groups. Follow these steps:

Prewriting

A. Choose one of the following topics and on a separate piece of paper do a prewriting activity such as clustering, freewriting, or brainstorming to generate some ideas about how to classify it.

- Types of mistakes people make when learning a second language
- Types of students
- Types of martial arts
- Kinds of bad habits
- Kinds of engineers (doctors, lawyers)
- Types of athletes
- Your choice

classify

3 groups

B. Using the ideas you generated in your prewriting activity, determine the most appropriate method of classification. Make sure your groups are separate and distinct. Then prepare an outline of your essay that includes your thesis statement and supporting ideas.

Writing

On a separate piece of paper, write the first draft of your essay. Refer to the essay plan on page 95 to help you write your draft. Be sure to provide some background information in the introduction and include a clear thesis statement. Organize the body of the essay so that you discuss one group in each supporting paragraph. End with a conclusion that restates the method of classification and summarizes the groups.

Revising and Editing

A. Personal Revising. Wait at least one day, and then revise your essay using the checklist on page 75. Write or type a revised version of your essay.

B. Peer Revising. Exchange drafts with a classmate. Use the following worksheet as a guide for suggesting improvements in your partner's essay.

Writer: _____ Peer Editor: _____

1. What technique did the author use in the introduction? _____
   _____
   _____

2. Was the technique effective? _____ yes _____ no

   If not, how can the introduction be improved? _____
   _____
   _____

3. Are the groups used in the classification separate _____ yes _____ no
   and distinct?

   If not, what is another way to classify the topic? _____
   _____
   _____

4. Did the author give an adequate description of
   each group? _____ yes _____ no

   If not, where is more information needed? _____
   _____
   _____

5. What are the strengths and weaknesses of the conclusion? _____
   _____
   _____

Incorporate any suggestions your partner has made that you agree with.

C. Editing. Use the checklist on page 56 to edit your essay. Correct all the grammar, punctuation, capitalization, and spelling errors before you copy it over or type it.

Explore the Web

Explore the Web to find out how musical instruments are classified. Use the information to make an informal outline of an essay about the classification of musical instruments.

You Be the Editor

The following classification paragraph describes the three types of consumer products. The content of the paragraph is correct, but there are nine mistakes. Find the mistakes and correct them. Then copy the corrected paragraph on a separate piece of paper.

Consumer products are usually divided into three groups, convenience, shopping, and specialty products. Each group is based on the way people buys products. Convenience products are products that a consumer needs but that he or she is not willing to spend very much time or effort shopping for. Convenience products usually inexpensive, frequently purchased items. Some common examples are bread, newspapers soda, and gasoline. Buyers spend few time planning the purchase of a convenience product. Also do not compare brands or sellers. The second group, shopping products, are those products that customers feel are worth the time and effort to compare with competing products. Furniture, refrigerators, cars, and televisions are examples of shopping products. Because these products are expected to last a long time. They are purchased less frequently than convenience products. The last group is specialty products. Specialty products are consumer products that the customer really wants and makes a special effort to find and buying. Buyers actually plan the purchase of a specialty product. They know what they want and will not accept a substitute. A high-tech camera, a pair of skis, and a haircut by a certain stylist are examples of specialty products. In searching for specialty products. Buyers do not compare alternatives.

On Your Own

Choose one of the following topics and write a classification essay. Make sure that your introduction gives the method of classification, identifies the groups, and states the purpose. Also, make sure that your groups are separate and distinct.

1. Types of magazines
2. Styles of architecture
3. Kinds of phobias
4. Your own topic

CHAPTER 7

Causes and Effects

Most people are curious. They want to know why something happened. They also want to know what happened as a result of some event or action. When you want to analyze the reasons (causes or factors) or the results (effects, disadvantages, benefits) of something, you should use a **cause** or **effect** type of essay. For example, when you answer a question such as, "Why did you decide to major in physics?" you are analyzing causes, and when you answer a question such as, "What effects will learning English have on your career?" you are analyzing effects.

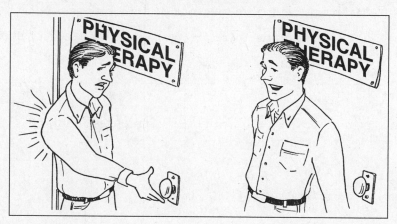

In academic writing, you will frequently need to examine causes and/or effects. For example, in a physiology class, you might need to discuss the common causes of chronic pain and the effects of physical therapy on patients who go through it. In a history class, you might be asked to analyze the technological causes of the Industrial Revolution or the effects of the Industrial Revolution on family life in England. In an economics class, you might be required to explain the reasons for the high inflation rate in Brazil or the effects of the high rate of inflation on the Brazilian middle class. In an anthropology course, you might need to explore the reasons why many of the world's languages are disappearing or the effects of their disappearance on indigenous populations.

The Language of Causes and Effects: Useful Phrases and Sentence Patterns

---

Transition Signals That Indicate a Cause or Effect Relationship

and that is why	It was raining, **and that is why** we canceled the soccer game.
as a consequence of	**As a consequence of** the rain, we canceled the soccer game.
as a result of	**As a result of** the rain, we canceled the soccer game.
because	**Because** it was raining, we canceled the soccer game.
because of	**Because of** the rain, we canceled the soccer game.
consequently	It was raining. **Consequently**, we canceled the soccer game.
due to	**Due to** the rain, we canceled the soccer game.
for this reason	It was raining. **For this reason**, we canceled the soccer game.
since	**Since** it was raining, we canceled the soccer game.
so	It was raining, **so** we canceled the soccer game.
therefore	It was raining; **therefore**, we canceled the soccer game.
thus	It was raining; **thus**, we canceled the soccer game.

The following sentence patterns are useful in writing topic sentences and thesis statements for cause or effect paragraphs and essays.

1. **There are several** | causes of
   | reasons for ____.
   | effects of

There are several causes of jet lag.

2. **There are** | three
   | four   **main reasons why** ____.
   | several

There are three main reasons why I want to get my own apartment.

3. **____ has had** | several
   | many   **important effects on** ____.
   | a few

My parents' divorce has had several important effects on my life.

Write a sample thesis statement for each of the following essay topics. Use a variety of the sentence patterns modeled on page 102.

1. Topic: The effects of unemployment

   Thesis statement: _____
   _____

2. Topic: The causes of depletion of the ozone layer

   Thesis statement: _____
   _____

3. Topic: The reasons you decided to learn English

   Thesis statement: _____
   _____

4. Topic: The effects of forest fires

   Thesis statement: _____
   _____

5. Topic: The effects of culture shock

   Thesis statement: _____
   _____

6. Topic: The reasons for eating a balanced diet

   Thesis statement: _____
   _____

DESCRIBING CAUSES AND EFFECTS

Look at the news photographs below and on page 105 and write sentences about causes or effects. Use a variety of expressions.

Example

a. __Many fish and water birds died because of the oil spill.__

b. __Due to the oil spill, sea life in this area has been devastated.__

c. __As a result of the oil spill, thousands of dead lobsters have washed__
__up on the beach.__

1.

a. _____

b. _____

c. _____

2.

a. _____

b. _____

c. _____

3.

a. _____

b. _____

c. _____

4.

a. _____

b. _____

c. _____

WRITING A PARAGRAPH ABOUT CAUSES

Read the following conversation between two friends.

MARK: Hi, Janie. How long have you been here?

JANIE: It seems like hours, but I actually didn't get here until 9:30. The lines are so long, and half the courses I wanted are already closed.

MARK: I'll bet you wish you'd preregistered.

JANIE: I sure do, but I was planning to change my major and I didn't know what courses I'd need this semester.

MARK: So, you've decided not to go into anthropology after all? What happened?

JANIE: I realized the job prospects weren't too good for an anthropologist with only a B.A. degree.

MARK: What about graduate school?

JANIE: I thought about that, but I really want to start working right after graduation. Maybe I'll go to grad school in a few years, but for now I want something more practical.

MARK: I can relate to that. That's why I'm majoring in engineering. Anyway, what department are you switching to?

JANIE: Believe it or not, I've decided to go into nursing.

MARK: That's great, but it'll be a big change after anthro.

JANIE: I know, but I've always liked working with people and helping others. When I was in high school, I did a lot of volunteer work at the local hospital.

MARK: Well, good luck with your new career. I guess we won't be in any of the same classes this semester.

Using information from the conversation, write a paragraph that describes the reasons Janie is changing her major. Be sure to include a topic sentence and transitions. Write your paragraph on a separate piece of paper.

ANALYZING AN ESSAY ABOUT CAUSES

The essay below discusses possible causes of the extinction of dinosaurs. Read the essay.

The Extinction of the Dinosaurs

For almost 140 million years, dinosaurs and other large reptiles ruled the land, sky, and sea. Dinosaurs came in sizes and shapes suited to every corner of the world. Then, approximately 65 million years ago, these huge reptiles died out and mammals took over the Earth. Few mysteries have ever excited the imaginations of scientists as much as this great extinction that killed off all the dinosaurs. Over the years, scientists have developed many theories to explain the causes of the disappearance of the dinosaurs and the other great reptiles. Three possible causes are a change in the Earth's climate, disease, and the Earth's collision with a large asteroid.

Some scientists believe that the number of dinosaurs declined and eventually disappeared due to a change in the Earth's climate. During the Cretaceous period the climate was tropical. Research indicates that at the end of the Cretaceous period the temperature dropped and the climate became much colder. For this reason, many of the plants that the plant-eating dinosaurs ate died. The death of the plants would cause many of the plant-eaters to die too. As the plant-eating dinosaurs died off, so did the meat-eaters

who fed on them. The colder climate may have caused problems for the dinosaurs in other ways, too. Because of their size, many dinosaurs were too big to hibernate in dens. They also lacked fur or feathers for protection against the cold. As a result, the dinosaurs were unable to adapt to the new cold conditions.

Another possible cause for the extinction of dinosaurs is disease. Some scientists think that diseases killed off the dinosaurs when large groups migrated across land bridges between the separate continents and infected one another with new illnesses. As the Cretaceous period went on, more and more land bridges started to appear on the Earth. Because the oceans were drying up and dinosaurs were able to walk across the land bridges, they began to spread new diseases.

A third cause for the extinction of dinosaurs is the asteroid theory. According to this theory, the extinction was much more sudden and catastrophic. In the late 1970s, scientists discovered evidence for the abrupt end to the Age of Dinosaurs. Dr. Louis Alvarez and his colleagues arrived at a revolutionary hypothesis to explain the extinction of dinosaurs. They suggested that about 65 million years ago, the Earth was struck by a huge asteroid. The asteroid was destroyed in the explosion, and billions of tons of dust were thrown up into the air. A thick cloud of dust blocked out sunlight for a long time. Consequently, plants were not able to make food, and they died. The lack of plants killed off many of the plant-eating dinosaurs, which then caused the death of the meat-eating dinosaurs that preyed on them. The darkness caused temperatures to fall below freezing for many months. As a result of this sudden change in climate, the dinosaur populations became smaller and smaller.

It seems that no one theory adequately explains why dinosaurs died out. Perhaps dinosaurs simply could not adjust to the changes that were taking place on the Earth toward the end of the Cretaceous period. Perhaps it was a combination of causes that contributed to the end of the Age of Dinosaurs.

Work with a Partner

Answer the following questions with a partner.

1. What three main causes does the author suggest to explain the extinction of the dinosaurs?
2. What techniques are used in the introduction and conclusion?
3. What cause or effect transitions did the author use to connect the ideas in the essay? Underline them.

ESSAY PLAN: CAUSE OR EFFECT

The guidelines below will help you remember what you need to do in each part of a cause or effect essay.

Introduction
1. Provide background information about the situation you are analyzing.
2. Describe the situation.
3. State whether you plan to discuss its causes or its effects.
4. Identify the main causes or effects.
5. Write a thesis statement that states the focus of your essay.

Supporting Paragraphs
1. State the first (second, third) cause or effect in the first (second, third) paragraph.
2. Support the first (second, third) cause or effect with facts, examples, statistics, or quotations.

Conclusion
1. Summarize the main causes or effects.
2. Draw a conclusion or make a prediction.

 When you write an essay you must think about how you are going to order the supporting paragraphs. Which paragraph should come first, second, and third? One common way is to organize the paragraphs according to order of importance. For example, in an essay about causes, you can begin with the most important cause and end with the least important cause.

Writing Essays about Causes

A. You are a reporter for a health magazine. Your assignment is to write an article on the topic of *the causes of heart disease.*

Prewriting

Read the assignment and discuss it with a partner.

You have just conducted an interview with a cardiologist, Dr. Harvey Snyder, and have written the following introduction:

> Heart disease affects so many people that it has become a serious concern for medical science. The heart is a complex organ that is vulnerable to hereditary as well as environmental risks. Cardiologists think of these risk factors as either major or minor causes of heart disease.

Dr. Snyder has identified a number of risk factors associated with heart disease. He has grouped these risk factors into major and minor causes. Here are your notes from the interview:

MAJOR CAUSES OF HEART DISEASE:

1. Family history—you are at a higher risk for developing heart disease if your parents or grandparents have had it.

2. High blood pressure—causes the heart to work too hard and can damage arteries.

3. High cholesterol levels—dangerous because fatty deposits build up in blood vessels.

4. Diabetes—can lead to hardening of the arteries and heart attacks.

5. Smoking cigarettes—smokers are two or three times more likely to have a heart attack than nonsmokers.

MINOR CAUSES OF HEART DISEASE:

1. Having a Type A personality—becoming easily stressed, being overly competitive, aggressive, and intense.

2. Having a sedentary lifestyle—not getting enough exercise.

3. Obesity—being extremely overweight and having a poor diet.

Writing

On a separate piece of paper, write a draft of two supporting paragraphs. Discuss the major causes of heart disease in one paragraph and the minor causes in the other paragraph. Also write a conclusion for your article. You might suggest ways to lessen the risks of heart disease by adopting a healthful lifestyle and good personal habits. Then copy your entire article, including the introduction, body, and conclusion, onto another sheet of paper.

Revising and Editing

Exchange drafts with a partner. Use the checklists on pages 56 and 75. Discuss any suggestions that your partner has for revision and editing. Make sure that your partner has provided enough support for each cause and that he or she has connected ideas with transitions. Write or type a revised version of your essay.

B. You are taking an introductory business course. You have been asked to analyze the following case and *determine the causes for the failure of a restaurant called the Undergrad Grill.*

Prewriting

In small groups read the case and study the drawings of Restaurant Row and the Undergrad Grill. Pay attention to the menu and the sign on the door of the Undergrad Grill.

On April 15, Tom Higgins opened a new restaurant at Benson University. He called it the Undergrad Grill. Tom had wanted to open a restaurant at Benson for several months but was waiting for the right location to become available. He was very pleased when he was able to rent suitable space on Restaurant Row. He figured that this would be a great location and well worth the high rent and all the renovations he needed to do on the building. Since he wanted to open the restaurant as soon as possible, he hired the first people he could find to do the renovations and painting. He ended up overpaying the workers because he wanted to get the job done as quickly as possible. When the time came to open, he didn't have enough money to do much advertising. However, since his restaurant was surrounded by many other restaurants and since over 25,000 undergraduate and graduate students were looking for a place to eat, Higgins was certain his restaurant would do well even without advertising. After placing several help-wanted ads in the local newspaper, Higgins hired two waitresses to work for him. He couldn't afford professional cooks, so he hired several students to do the cooking.

Unfortunately for Higgins, the competition was more intense than he had anticipated. After two months, his restaurant was doing poorly. One of his waitresses had quit and the number of customers was decreasing.

UNDERGRAD GRILL

▼▲▼▲▼▲▼▲▼▲▼▲▼▲▼▲▼▲▼▲▼▲▼▲▼▲▼▲

Open 11 A.M. to 11 P.M.

UNDERGRAD GRILL

NO Bare feet
NO Smoking
NO Skateboards
NO Children
   under Age 5
NO take out

Soups

Hot and sour	$ 4.00
Black bean	$ 4.00
French onion	$ 4.00
Wonton	$ 4.00
Vegetable	$ 4.00

Entrées

Hamburger	$ 8.95
Cheeseburger	$10.95
Fried chicken	$ 9.95
Filet of fish	$ 6.95
Chicken fajita	$ 8.95
Beef fajita	$10.95
Shrimp tempura	$10.95
Pork fried rice	$ 6.95
Steak au poivre	$12.95
Spaghetti and meatballs	$ 7.95
Chicken and hummus	$ 8.95
Lamb curry	$14.95

Vegetables & Side Dishes

Baked potato	$ 3.00
French fries	$ 3.00
Rice	$ 3.00
Corn on the cob (in season)	$ 3.00
Peas	$ 3.00
Green beans	$ 3.00
House salad	$ 4.50

Desserts

Homemade apple pie	$ 5.00
Chocolate mousse	$ 5.00
Flan	$ 5.00
Ice cream	$ 4.00
Mixed fresh fruit	$ 3.50

Drinks

Lemonade	$ 4.00
Coffee	$ 3.00
Tea	$ 3.00
Soda	$ 2.00

Credit cards accepted. No checks.

Talk about why you think the restaurant is doing poorly. Make a list of the causes for the failure of the restaurant.

1. _____

2. _____

3. _____

4. _____

5. _____

6. _____

Work independently. Use your list to write an essay about the reasons (causes) the Undergrad Grill is doing poorly.

Revising and Editing

Revise your essay using the Revising Checklist on page 75 and the Editing Checklist on page 56. Also, check to make sure that you have provided enough support to fully describe each cause. Write or type a revised version of your essay.

Writing an Essay about Effects

In this activity, you will practice writing an essay about effects. Follow these steps:

Prewriting

A. Choose one of the following topics and do a prewriting activity such as clustering, freewriting, or brainstorming to generate some ideas.

- The effects of divorce on family life
- The effects of a natural disaster such as an earthquake or hurricane
- The effects of climate on lifestyle
- The effects of a social, political, or economic problem in a country you are familiar with
- The effects that your peers have had on you

B. Using the ideas you generated in your prewriting activity, identify several major effects and prepare an outline of your essay.

**READY
TO WRITE**

Writing

On a separate piece of paper, write the first draft of your essay. Use the essay plan on page 108 to help you write your draft. Be sure to provide some background information about your topic in the introduction and include a clear thesis statement that states its main effects. Organize the body paragraphs according to order of importance, with the most important effect last. End with a conclusion that summarizes the main effects, draws a conclusion, or makes a prediction.

Revising and Editing

A. Personal Revising. Wait at least one day, and then revise your essay using the checklist on page 75. Write or type a revised version of your essay. Also, check to make sure that you have provided enough support to fully describe each effect. Write or type a revised version of your essay.

B. Peer Revising. Exchange drafts with a classmate. Use the following worksheet as a guide for suggesting improvements in your partner's essay.

Writer: _____   Peer Editor: _____

1. Does the introduction provide enough background   _____ yes _____ no
   information to interest you in the topic?

   If not, how can it be improved? _____

   _____

   _____

2. Are the paragraphs arranged in a logical order   _____ yes _____ no
   within the essay?

   If not, how can the order be improved? _____

   _____

   _____

3. Does each body paragraph provide enough   _____ yes _____ no
   support for each effect?

4. Are the sentences arranged in a logical   _____ yes _____ no
   order within each body paragraph?

   If not, how can the order be improved? _____

   _____

   _____

5. What are the strengths and weaknesses of the conclusion? _____

   _____

   _____

Incorporate any suggestions your partner has made that you agree with.

C. Editing. Use the checklist on page 56 to edit your essay. Correct all the grammar, punctuation, capitalization, and spelling errors before you copy it over or type it.

Explore the Web

Choose an important historical event in the history of your country. Explore the Web to find the causes or effects of the event. Make a list and share the information you gather with your classmates.

You Be the Editor

The paragraph that follows discusses the effects of the Great Depression. The content of the paragraph is correct, but there are ten mistakes. Find the mistakes and correct them. Then copy the corrected paragraph on a separate piece of paper.

The Great Depression of the 1930s affected Americans for generations. The complete collapse of the stock market began on October 24 1929, when 13 million shares of stock were sold. On Tuesday, October 29, known as Black Tuesday, more than 16 million shares were sold. The value of most shares fell sharply, resulting in financial ruin for many people and widespread panic through the country. Although there have been other financial panics. None has had such a devastating and long-term effect as the Great Depression. By 1932, the industrial output of the United States had been cut in half. One-fourth of the labor force, about 15 million people, was out of work, and hourly wages dropped almost 50 percent. In addition, hundreds of banks will fail. Prices for agricultural products dropped to their lowest level since the Civil War. More than 90,000 businesses failed complete. Statistics, however, cannot tell the story of the extraordinary hardships the masses of americans suffered. For nearly every unemployed people, there were dependents who needed to be fed and housed. People in the United States had never known such massive poverty and hunger before. Former millionaires stood on street corners trying to selling apples at 5 cents apiece. Thousands lose their homes. Because they could not pay there mortgages. Some people moved in with relatives. Others moved to shabby sections of town and built shelters out of tin cans and cardboard. Homeless people slept outside under old newspapers. Many Americans waited in lines in every city, hoping for something to eat. Unfortunately, many of these people died of malnutrition. In 1931 alone, more than 20,000 Americans committed suicide.

On Your Own

Choose one of the following general subjects and brainstorm a list of its causes or effects. Using the ideas generated from your list, write an essay about causes or effects.

1. An important historical event in your country
2. The explosion of the Internet
3. Getting good grades
4. Getting married or divorced
5. Your own topic

CHAPTER 8

Comparison/Contrast

Very often in your writing, you will want to show how ideas, people, or things are similar or different. In these cases, you will use a **comparison/contrast** type of essay. When you **compare** two things, you look for how they are similar. When you **contrast** two things, you look for how they are different. It is important that the two things you compare or contrast belong to the same general class. For example, you probably would not want to compare or contrast a house and a dog. You could, however, compare and contrast a Japanese house and a North American house.

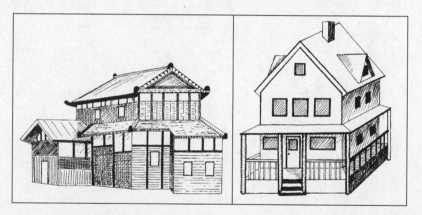

In academic writing, comparison and contrast are often used to support a point or persuade the reader. For example, in a political science class, you might compare and contrast two leaders in order to prove which one was more successful at bringing about economic reforms. In a literature class, you might compare and contrast two short stories to show which one you liked better. In an engineering class, you might compare and contrast two methods of combustion to explain why one is more efficient than the other.

The Language of Comparison and Contrast: Useful Phrases and Sentence Patterns

Comparison

and . . . too	Tokyo has an efficient subway system, **and** London does **too**.
as . . . as	Tokyo's subway system is **as** efficient **as** London's.
likewise	Tokyo has an efficient subway system. **Likewise**, London has an efficient subway system.
similarly	Tokyo has an efficient subway system. **Similarly**, London has an efficient subway system.
alike	New York City and Tokyo are **alike** in several ways.
both . . . and	**Both** Japan **and** Korea are in Asia.
like	The weather in Philadelphia is **like** the weather in Istanbul.
similar to	The population of Vienna is **similar to** the population of Frankfurt.
the same	Philadelphia has **the same** kind of weather as Istanbul.
the same as	The altitude of Calcutta is **the same as** the altitude of Copenhagen.

Contrast

but	The Sahara desert has a dry climate, **but** the Amazon rain forest has a wet climate.
different from	The climate in the Sahara desert is very **different from** the climate in the Amazon rain forest.
however	The Sahara desert has a dry climate. **However**, the Amazon rain forest has a wet climate.
in contrast	The Sahara desert has a dry climate. **In contrast**, the Amazon rain forest has a wet climate.
on the other hand	The Sahara desert has a dry climate. **On the other hand**, the Amazon rain forest has a wet climate.
while	**While** the Sahara desert is dry, the Amazon rain forest is wet.
whereas	**Whereas** the Sahara desert is dry, the Amazon rain forest is wet.
unlike	**Unlike** rain forests, deserts get very little rain.
although	**Although** the Sahara desert has a dry climate, some crops can be grown there.
even though	**Even though** the Sahara desert has a dry climate, some crops can be grown there.

The following sentence patterns are useful in writing topic sentences and thesis statements for comparison/contrast essays and paragraphs:

1. **There are several** │ differences **between** ____ and ____.
   │ similarities

*There are several differences **between** high school **and** college.*

*There are several similarities **between** high school **and** college.*

2. ____ **and** ____ **are** │ similar **in many ways.**
   │ different

*Thai food **and** Vietnamese food **are** similar **in many ways.***

*Thai food **and** Vietnamese food **are** different **in many ways.***

3. ____ **is** │ different from ____ **in many ways.**
   │ similar to

*My father **is** different from his older brother **in many ways.***

*My father **is** similar to his older brother **in many ways.***

4. ____ **and** ____ **have** │ several **things in common.**
   │ many

*My best friend **and** I **have** several **things in common.***

5. **A comparison between** ____ **and** ____ │ reveals
   │ shows ____.
   │ demonstrates

A comparison between jazz and rock 'n' roll reveals some surprising similarities.

A comparison between jazz and rock 'n' roll reveals some surprising differences.

Write a sample thesis statement for a comparison/contrast essay on each of the following topics. Use a variety of the sentence patterns modeled above.

1. Topic: Chinese food and Mexican food

   Thesis statement: _____

2. Topic: Soccer and basketball

   Thesis statement: _____

3. Topic: Capitalism and communism

   Thesis statement: _____

4. Topic: American cars and Japanese cars

   Thesis statement: _____

5. Topic: Two of your classmates

   Thesis statement: _____

Examining Comparisons and Contrasts

Look at the following two classified ads for apartments for rent. Find several similarities and differences between the two apartments. Write two sentences of comparison and two sentences of contrast.

1.

Apartments for Rent

Large 2-bedroom apt., 2 bathrooms, eat-in kitchen, large living room, air-conditioning, wall-to-wall carpeting, great location on Monument Street, NO pets, $700/month, all utilities included. Call Mr. Toll at (315) 446–3377.

Huron Towers: 10th floor—great view of river, **3 bedrooms**, 2 bathrooms, modern kitchen with new appliances, fireplace in living room, hardwood floors, air-conditioning, laundry facilities, utilities NOT included. NO pets. Pool and tennis courts on premises. $995/month. Call for appointment: (315) 885–3909.

Example

a. <u>The apartment on Monument Street has fewer bedrooms than the apartment in Huron Towers.</u>

b. _____

c. _____

d. _____

Now do the same for the next two sets of classified ads.

2.

Used Cars for Sale

2001 Toyota Camry. Automatic transmission. Excellent condition. Fully loaded. 18,000 miles. Gray leather interior, dark green exterior. ABS brakes. Sun roof. Driver's side air bag. CD player. $21,000. Call (413) 248–5573.

2000 Audi Quattro. Mint condition. Standard transmission. 25,000 miles. Loaded. Silver with black leather interior. Sun roof. ABS brakes. Seat heaters. Tape deck. Dual air bags. Theft alarm system. $28,000. Call (508) 427–0511.

a. _____

b. _____

c. _____

d. _____

3.

PETS

| Golden Retriever puppy for sale. 5-month-old male. Great with kids. One-year health guarantee. $100. Call (617) 368–3254. | German Shepherd puppy needs home. Female, 7 months. House-trained. Excellent watch dog. Health guarantee for first year. $100. Call (617) 576–3124 after 6 P.M. |

a. _____

b. _____

c. _____

d. _____

Writing about Comparisons

You are studying the impact of heredity on human behavior and are doing research on identical twins who were separated at birth. The paragraph below is the introductory paragraph you have written for your report.

Some of the most important research in the field of behavioral genetics comes from the studies of identical twins who were separated at birth. Dr. Thomas J. Bouchard is a professor at the University of Minnesota who has conducted many influential studies on identical twins. He believes that by examining their differences and similarities, we will better understand the mysteries of heredity and environment. One of the most revealing pair of twins that Dr. Bouchard has studied is known as "the Jim twins." Jim Springer and Jim Lewis are identical twins who were separated at birth because their 14-year-old mother could not take care of them. They were not reunited until 39 years later. According to Dr. Bouchard, the Jim twins are "the most valuable pair that has ever been studied" because the similarities between them are so astounding.

Source: *Good Housekeeping*

On a separate piece of paper, write a paragraph on the similarities between Jim Springer and Jim Lewis. The following is a list of the similarities that you have gathered. There are too many similarities listed here for one paragraph. Choose the ones that you think are the most interesting to include in your paragraph. Remember to begin your paragraph with a clearly stated topic sentence.

- Each brother was told that his brother had died at birth.
- Both brothers are emotional, sentimental, kind, generous, friendly, and loving by nature.
- Neither brother gets angry easily, and if he does get angry, he doesn't show it.
- Both bite their fingernails and/or jiggle one foot when nervous.

- They look exactly alike.
- They are both 6 feet tall and weigh 180 pounds.
- They walk the same way.
- Both cross their legs the same way.
- Their voices sound exactly the same.
- They use the same gestures when they speak.
- Both use the same expressions, such as "Mama mía" and "Cool."
- Both enjoy woodworking and have built several birdhouses and tables.
- Both brothers are poor spellers.
- Both were married first to women named Linda.
- Their second wives were both named Betty.
- As children, they each had a dog and named it Toy.
- They have both taken family vacations on the same beach in Florida.
- Until they were reunited, each had felt an emptiness, as though something was missing from his life.
- Jim Springer named his son James Allen; Jim Lewis named his son James Alan.
- Both frequently buy gifts (that they cannot afford) for their wives.
- Both men have worked part time in law enforcement.

Now revise and edit your paragraph. Copy it over and give it to your teacher.

METHODS OF ORGANIZATION FOR COMPARISON AND CONTRAST

There are two basic patterns for writing a comparison/contrast essay: the **block method** and the **point-by-point method**.

In the block method, you describe all the similarities in the first supporting paragraph and then all the differences in the second supporting paragraph.

In the point-by-point method, you identify several important points to be compared and contrasted. In the first supporting paragraph, you compare and contrast the two things according to the first point. In the second supporting paragraph, you compare and contrast the two things according to the second point, and so on. Most student writers find the block method easier to master.

Analyzing Essays of Comparison and Contrast

Read the following two essays. The purpose of both essays is to explain why a student chose to attend Greenwell University rather than State University.

Essay 1

Last week when I received acceptances from my top two choices for college, State and Greenwell, I knew I had a difficult decision to make.

Although I had talked to friends and relatives who had attended both schools and had visited both campuses many times, I couldn't make up my mind. It was only after I analyzed the similarities and differences between the two schools that I finally came to my decision to begin classes at Greenwell in the fall.

At first glance, it seems that State and Greenwell have a lot in common. First of all, both universities are located in Pennsylvania, where I am from. The tuition is also exactly the same at both schools—$20,000 per year. In addition, the basketball team at State is just as good as the one at Greenwell, and I would love to play for either one. Most importantly, both schools have large libraries, excellent academic reputations, and first-class engineering departments.

It was when I looked at the differences between the two schools that I made my final decision. In terms of location, State is more attractive. Its setting in a safe suburb was definitely more appealing than Greenwell's location in a dangerous city neighborhood. I also liked State's older campus with its beautiful buildings and trees more than Greenwell's new campus, which looks like an office complex. But I realized that these should not be the most important factors in my decision. I had to pay a lot of attention to the financial component. Although the tuition is the same at both schools, Greenwell offered me a $3,000 scholarship, whereas State couldn't give me any financial aid. In addition, if I go to Greenwell, I can live at home and save money on room and board. Since Greenwell is much closer to home, I won't have to spend as much on transportation to and from school. The most important factor in making my decision was the difference in class size between the two universities. State has large classes and an impersonal feeling. On the other hand, Greenwell has small classes, and students get a lot of personal attention.

In conclusion, after taking everything into consideration, I think I made the right decision. Since small classes, personal attention from my professors, and saving money are all very important to me, I will probably be happier at Greenwell.

Answer the following questions with a partner.

1. What method did the author of this essay use?

   _____

2. What is the thesis statement?

   _____

3. What is the topic sentence of the first supporting paragraph?

   _____

4. What similarities between the two schools does the author mention?

   _____

   _____

   _____

5. What is the topic sentence of the second supporting paragraph?

   _____

6. What differences between the two schools does the author mention?

   _____

   _____

   _____

   _____

Essay 2

Last week when I received acceptances from my top two choices for college, State and Greenwell, I knew I had a difficult decision to make. Although I had talked to friends and relatives who had attended both schools and had visited both campuses many times, I couldn't make up my mind. It was only after I compared the location, cost, and quality of education of the two schools that I could finally come to my decision to attend Greenwell.

The first thing I considered was the location. First of all, both universities are located in Pennsylvania, where I am from. But that is where the similarities end. State's setting in a safe suburb is definitely more appealing than Greenwell's location in a dangerous city neighborhood. I also like State's older campus with its beautiful buildings and gardens more than Greenwell's new campus, which looks like an office complex.

In addition to location, I had to pay a lot of attention to the financial component. The tuition is the same at both schools—$20,000 per year. However, Greenwell offered me a $3,000 scholarship, but State couldn't give me any money. Also, if I go to Greenwell, I can live at home and save money on room and board. Finally, since Greenwell is much closer to home, I won't have to spend as much on transportation to and from school.

The quality of education at the two schools had the most influence on my decision. In many ways, State and Greenwell have similar standards of education. Both schools have large libraries and excellent academic reputations. Also, State has a first-class engineering department, and so does Greenwell. So I had to look at other things. What it came down to was the difference in class size between the two universities. State has large classes and an impersonal feeling. On the other hand, Greenwell has small classes, and students get a lot of personal attention.

In conclusion, after taking everything into consideration, I think I made the right decision. Since small classes, saving money, and personal attention from my professors are very important to me, I will probably be happier at Greenwell.

Work with a Partner

Answer the following questions with a partner.

1. What method did the author of this essay use?

   _____

2. What is the thesis statement?

   _____

3. What three points about the schools did the author compare and contrast?

   _____

   _____

   _____

4. How did the author organize the order of the supporting paragraphs within the essay? Least important to most important? Or most important to least important?

   _____

5. What transitions did the author use to connect the ideas in the essay? Underline them.

Essay Plans: Comparison/Contrast

Block Method

The guidelines below will help you remember what you need to do in each part of a comparison/contrast essay using the block method.

Introduction

1. Provide background information about your topic.
2. Identify the two things being compared and contrasted.
3. State the purpose for making the comparison and/or contrast.
4. Write a thesis statement that states the focus of your essay.

Supporting Paragraphs

1. In the first paragraph(s), discuss the similarities.
2. In the next paragraph(s), discuss the differences.

Conclusion

1. Restate the purpose for comparison and/or contrast in different words.
2. Summarize the main similarities and differences.
3. Draw a conclusion.

Point-by-Point Method

The guidelines below will help you remember what you need to do in each section of a comparison/contrast essay using the point-by-point method.

Introduction

1. Provide background information about your topic.
2. Identify the two things being compared and contrasted.
3. State the purpose for making the comparison and/or contrast.
4. Identify the points to be compared and contrasted.
5. Write a thesis statement that states the focus of your essay.

Supporting Paragraphs

1. In the first paragraph, compare and/or contrast the two things according to the first point you identified.
2. In the second paragraph, compare and/or contrast the two things according to the second point you identified.
3. Do the same thing in the third and subsequent paragraphs.

Conclusion

1. Restate the purpose for comparison and/or contrast in different words.
2. Summarize the main similarities and differences.
3. Draw a conclusion.

TIP When you use the point-by-point method to write about similarities or differences, you need to decide how you are going to order the points. Again, one common way is to organize the points according to order of importance. For example, you can begin with the most important point and end with the least important point.

Writing an Essay of Comparison and Contrast: Block Method

In this activity, you will practice writing an essay of comparison and contrast. Follow these steps:

Prewriting

A. Choose one of the following topics and use the space below to brainstorm a list of similarities and differences.

- Compare and contrast yourself and another member of your family.
- Compare and contrast some aspect of your culture, such as eating habits, education, government, economy, religion, or social life, with the same aspect of another culture.
- Compare and contrast a photo and a painting of the same scene.
- Compare and contrast two people you have worked with, such as two co-workers at a job, two students in a group, two secretaries you have known, or two bosses you have had.
- Your own topic

B. Organize your list by grouping the similarities in one group and the differences in another group. Then prepare an informal outline for your essay. Be sure that you have identified a purpose for making your comparison. For example, are you comparing two restaurants so that you can recommend one of them to a friend? Are you comparing your native language and English to show why English is easy or difficult for you to learn? Develop your essay according to your purpose.

Writing

On a separate piece of paper, write the first draft of your essay. Use the essay plan on page 124 to help you write your draft. Be sure to provide some background information in the introduction and include a clear thesis statement that states your purpose for comparison. Organize the supporting paragraphs so that all the similarities are in one paragraph and all the differences are in another paragraph. End with a conclusion that restates your purpose for the comparison and that summarizes the main similarities and differences.

**READY
TO WRITE**

A. Personal Revising. Wait at least one day, and then revise your essay using the checklist on page 75. Also, check to make sure you have provided enough support to explain fully the similarities and differences. Write or type a revised version of your essay.

B. Peer Revising. Exchange drafts with a partner. Use the following worksheet as a guide for suggesting improvements in your partner's essay.

Writer: _____ Peer Editor: _____

1. Did the introduction identify the two items being compared? _____ yes _____ no

2. Is the purpose of the comparison clearly stated? _____ yes _____ no

3. Did the introduction make you want to read the rest of the essay? _____ yes _____ no

   Why or why not? _____

   _____

   _____

4. Did the author adequately develop the points of comparison in a paragraph? _____ yes _____ no

   If not, how can the paragraph be strengthened? _____

   _____

   _____

5. Did the author adequately develop the points of contrast in another paragraph? _____ yes _____ no

   If not, how can the paragraph be strengthened? _____

   _____

   _____

6. Did the author include an effective conclusion? _____ yes _____ no

   If not, how can it be improved? _____

   _____

   _____

Incorporate any suggestions your partner has made that you agree with.

C. Editing. Use the checklist on page 56 to edit your essay. Correct all the grammar, punctuation, capitalization, and spelling errors before you copy it over or type it.

Explore the Web

Think of something you would like to buy such as a new television, car, sewing machine, camera, etc. Explore the Web to find two examples of that product that you could purchase on the Internet. Read the descriptions of the two items and make a list of the similarities and differences between them. For example, you can compare and contrast the price, size, quality, and features of the two items.

You Be the Editor

The following paragraph contains nine mistakes. Find the mistakes and correct them. Then copy the corrected paragraph onto a separate sheet of paper.

Now that I am pregnant with our first child, my husband and I will have to find a bigger place to live. Our little apartment in the city is too small for three people. We trying to decide whether we should get a biggest apartment in the city or move to the suburbs. We have four main considerations expense, space, convenience, and schools. In general, is probably expensiver to live in the city. On the other hand, we would have to buy a car if we moved to the suburbs we would also have to buy a lawnmower and a snowblower or hire someone care for the lawn and driveway. In terms of space, we could definitely have a bigger house and much more land if we lived in the suburbs. However, we wonder if it would be worth it, since we would lose so many conveniences. Stores would be farther away, and so would friends, neighbors, movie theaters, museums, and restaurants. The most biggest inconvenience would be that we would both have to commute to work every day instead of walking or taking the bus. The Schools are probably better in the suburbs, but for our child, who isn't even born yet, school is several years away. In looking at our priorities, it becomes clear that we should continue to live in the city for now and then reevaluate our decision as the baby gets closer to school age.

On Your Own

Write a comparison/contrast essay using the point-by-point method. Choose one of the topics below and identify several points on which to base your comparison. Follow the five steps of good writing as you write your essay, and be sure that you have a clear purpose for your comparison.

1. Compare and contrast two items such as a computer and a typewriter, glasses and contact lenses, a CD and a cassette tape, or a VCR and a DVD.
2. Compare and contrast dating customs in your generation and your grandparents' generation.
3. Your own topic

CHAPTER 9

Problem/Solution

When your purpose is to describe a problem and evaluate possible solutions, you will write a **problem/solution** essay. For example, if you are discussing solutions to the problem of employee dissatisfaction in your company or the problems of adjusting to a foreign culture, you would write this type of essay. You should organize your solutions according to order of importance.

The problem/solution pattern is very useful in academic writing. For example, you would use it in a sociology class if you were asked to talk about solutions to the problem of teen pregnancy. You could also write this type of essay in an economics class if you needed to suggest some ways to solve the unemployment problem in your city.

Brainstorming Solutions

For each of the problems described below, think of at least three possible solutions. Work in small groups, and then compare your solutions with those of your classmates.

1. Living in a foreign country can be fun and exciting, but it can also be problematic. One of the most serious problems that people living in a foreign country face is culture shock. What ways can you think of to help people deal with this problem?

   Problem: Culture shock

   Solutions:

   a. <u>Keep in touch with your family and friends at home.</u>

   b. _____

   c. _____

2. Many people have trouble falling asleep or staying asleep for an adequate amount of time. This problem is known as insomnia. What suggestions would you give to people who cannot seem to get a good night's sleep?

Problem: Insomnia

Solutions:

a. _____

b. _____

c. _____

3. Stress at work or school can be a serious problem. A person suffering from too much stress usually finds it difficult to be productive or happy. What are some ways to reduce the amount of stress in someone's life?

Problem: Stress at work or school

Solutions:

a. _____

b. _____

c. _____

4. The population of the world keeps growing. Every fifteen seconds, approximately 100 babies are born. Experts predict that by the year 2015, there will be 7 billion people on our planet. By the end of the century, the population could reach 10 billion people. The problem is that there probably will not be enough food to feed everyone. What solutions can you come up with to help solve this problem?

Problem: Overpopulation

Solutions:

a. _____

b. _____

c. _____

5. Crime is a serious problem in many large cities. Look back at the introduction to an essay on crime on page 65. Is crime a serious problem in the large cities in your native country? What solutions can you think of to reduce the amount of crime?

    Problem: Crime in large cities in the United States (or another country)

    Solutions:

    a. _____

    b. _____

    c. _____

6. Illiteracy is a serious problem all over the world. For example, one-third of adults in the United States are functionally illiterate. People who cannot read and write have many disadvantages functioning in society. What solutions can you come up with to help overcome this problem?

    Problem: Illiteracy

    Solutions:

    a. _____

    b. _____

    c. _____

7. Many of the Earth's resources are nonrenewable and will eventually run out. In order to make our valuable natural resources last longer, we need to conserve materials and recycle them as much as possible. Unfortunately, it is not always easy to convince people of the necessity of recycling. What ideas do you have about getting people to recycle?

    Problem: Getting people to recycle

    Solutions:

    a. _____

    b. _____

    c. _____

Offering Solutions

You are the advice consultant for a newspaper. How would you respond to the following letters? Be sure to offer several solutions to each problem in your response. Share your responses by exchanging papers with your classmates or by reading them out loud.

Dear Advisor,

When I first came to the United States to study Western literature, I never dreamed I would fall in love—especially with an American. I had planned to spend two years here getting my master's degree and then return to Japan and teach. Now, only nine months later, everything has changed. I met Jim in one of my classes, and we started studying together. One thing led to the next, and before I knew it, I was engaged. It wasn't exactly love at first sight, but almost. Jim's parents are wonderful. They say that they would love to have a Japanese daughter-in-law. Unfortunately, my parents are a different story. They can't accept the fact that I would marry someone who isn't Japanese. They are very upset and want me to forget about Jim and all our plans for a wedding when we graduate. In fact, they are urging me to come home at the end of the semester and spend the summer in Japan. They think that I'll get over Jim if I don't see him for three months.

I'm so confused. I'm really close to my parents and don't want to hurt them. On the other hand, I love Jim and want to spend the rest of my life with him. I think I would be happy living in the United States, but I'm afraid my parents would never get over it. What suggestions do you have for me? HELP!!

Confused

Dear Confused,

_____

_____

_____

_____

_____

_____

Dear Advisor,

I'm a sophomore in college. Last year my roommate, Fred, and I were very good friends. I don't know what happened, but this year everything has changed. Fred seems really different. He has a whole new group of friends and spends all of his time with them. He stays out late at night and often doesn't get up in time for his classes. He never studies any more, and he got kicked off the wrestling team for missing so many practices. He's always either sleeping or out with his new friends. When he's in our room, he is moody, messy, and undependable. Please tell me what to do. I've tried talking to him, but he just tells me to mind my own business. I'm concerned that he's going to get kicked out of school. He's already on academic probation. What should I do?

A Concerned Roommate

Dear Concerned,

_____

_____

_____

_____

_____

_____

Work with a Partner

On a separate piece of paper, write your own letter to the advice consultant. You can write about a real problem that you have or make one up. Then exchange letters with a classmate and write a response.

**READY
TO WRITE**

Read the essay below.

Energy Sources: A Dilemma for the Twenty-First Century

All of us have come to expect that reliable sources of energy will be available forever. We drive our cars wherever and whenever we want. When the gas tank gets low, we simply pull into the nearest gas station. At home, whenever we need to change the temperature, prepare food, listen to music, or watch TV, we simply turn on the nearest appliance. What is the source of all this energy that we use so carelessly? In most of the world, energy is created by burning fossil fuels—coal, natural gas, and oil. The problem is that these resources are finite. At our current rate of use, by the year 2080, the world's supply of oil will be almost gone. That means that if you are under the age of forty, the day will probably come when you will not have *enough* gasoline for your car or electricity for your appliances. The three most commonly proposed solutions to this worldwide problem are increasing the efficiency of appliances and vehicles, improving conservation efforts, and finding alternative energy sources.

The first solution, increasing the efficiency of appliances and vehicles, is something that manufacturers have been working on for three decades. For instance, televisions now use 65 to 75 percent less electricity than they did in the 1970s, refrigerators use 20 to 30 percent less electricity, and cars need less gas to travel more miles. Unfortunately, there are so many more televisions, refrigerators, and cars in the world now that overall consumption continues to rise.

Another solution to the dangerous energy situation is to improve our conservation efforts. For example, all of us must get in the habit of recycling whatever we can. We have to install high-efficiency light bulbs in our homes and offices and turn off the lights in rooms that we are not using. It would also help if we biked, walked, carpooled, or used public transportation more and used our cars less. Unfortunately, improvements in both conservation and efficiency are only temporary solutions. They extend the useful life of our current fuels, but they do not explain what we will do when these fuels run out.

The best solution, then, is to find alternative sources of energy to meet our future needs. The current leading alternatives to fossil fuels are fusion and solar energy. Fusion is a nuclear reaction that results in an enormous release of energy. It is practically pollution-free and is probably our best long-range option. Unfortunately, it will not be available for at least twenty years. The other possible energy source, solar power, is the source of all energy, except nuclear, on Earth. When people think of solar energy, they generally think of the many ways that individual homeowners can utilize the power of the sun for heating water and buildings. But solar energy can also be utilized to generate electricity and to purify fuels for automobiles.

It is clear that for us to have sufficient energy resources for the twenty-first century, it will be necessary to pursue the development and encourage the use of alternative energy sources worldwide. If we ignore this problem, what will become of our children? What will life be like for them in the year 2050?

Work with a Partner

Answer the following questions with a partner.

1. What is the thesis statement of the essay?
2. What three solutions to the energy shortage does the author propose?
3. What examples does the author use to describe each solution?
4. How are the supporting paragraphs arranged within the essay?
5. What technique(s) did the author use in writing the conclusion?

Essay Plan: Problem/Solution

The guidelines below will help you remember what you need to do in each part of a problem/solution essay.

Introduction

1. Describe the problem and state why it is serious.
2. Write a thesis statement that identifies possible solutions.

Supporting Paragraphs

1. Discuss one solution in each supporting paragraph.
2. Provide details to explain each solution.
3. Organize the paragraphs according to order of importance.

Conclusion

1. Summarize the solutions.
2. Draw a conclusion or make a prediction based on your suggestions.

Writing Problem/Solution Essays

Reread the case below about Tom Higgins's restaurant, The Undergrad Grill. In the Chapter 7 activity, you focused on the causes of the restaurant's problems. In this activity, you will focus on solutions.

On April 15, Tom Higgins opened a new restaurant at Benson University. He called it the Undergrad Grill. Tom had wanted to open a restaurant at Benson for several months but was waiting for the right location to become available. He was very pleased when he was able to rent suitable space on Restaurant Row. He figured that this would be a great location and well worth the high rent and all the renovations he needed to do on the building. Since he wanted to open the restaurant as soon as possible, he hired the first people he could find to do the renovations and painting. He ended up overpaying the workers because he wanted to get the job done as quickly as possible.

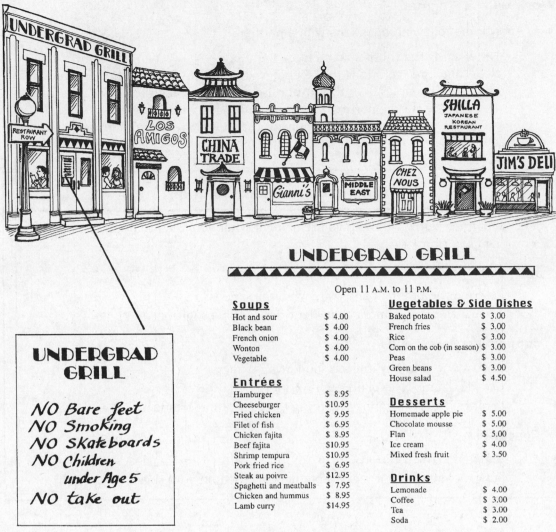

UNDERGRAD GRILL

NO Bare feet
NO Smoking
NO Skateboards
NO Children
    under Age 5
NO take out

UNDERGRAD GRILL

Open 11 A.M. to 11 P.M.

Soups

Hot and sour	$ 4.00
Black bean	$ 4.00
French onion	$ 4.00
Wonton	$ 4.00
Vegetable	$ 4.00

Entrées

Hamburger	$ 8.95
Cheeseburger	$10.95
Fried chicken	$ 9.95
Filet of fish	$ 6.95
Chicken fajita	$ 8.95
Beef fajita	$10.95
Shrimp tempura	$10.95
Pork fried rice	$ 6.95
Steak au poivre	$12.95
Spaghetti and meatballs	$ 7.95
Chicken and hummus	$ 8.95
Lamb curry	$14.95

Vegetables & Side Dishes

Baked potato	$ 3.00
French fries	$ 3.00
Rice	$ 3.00
Corn on the cob (in season)	$ 3.00
Peas	$ 3.00
Green beans	$ 3.00
House salad	$ 4.50

Desserts

Homemade apple pie	$ 5.00
Chocolate mousse	$ 5.00
Flan	$ 5.00
Ice cream	$ 4.00
Mixed fresh fruit	$ 3.50

Drinks

Lemonade	$ 4.00
Coffee	$ 3.00
Tea	$ 3.00
Soda	$ 2.00

Credit cards accepted. No checks.

When the time came to open, he didn't have enough money to do much advertising. However, since his restaurant was surrounded by many other restaurants and since over 25,000 undergraduate and graduate students were looking for a place to eat, Higgins was certain his restaurant would do well even without advertising. After placing several help-wanted ads in the local newspaper, Higgins hired two waitresses to work for him. He couldn't afford professional cooks, so he hired several students to do the cooking.

Unfortunately for Higgins, the competition was more intense than he had anticipated. After two months, his restaurant was doing poorly. One of his waitresses had quit and the number of customers was decreasing.

Work with a partner and brainstorm a list of solutions to Tom Higgins's problem.

Solutions

1. _____

2. _____

3. _____

4. _____

5. _____

6. _____

Writing

Use the list to plan and write an essay about solutions to Tom Higgins's problem. Choose several of the solutions on your list to develop into topics for the supporting paragraphs. Write an introduction that states the problem in a few sentences. End with a thesis statement that states the solutions you are going to discuss. Then write the supporting paragraphs using one solution for each paragraph. Finally, write a conclusion that leaves your reader thinking about the solutions.

Revising and Editing

Exchange drafts with a classmate. Discuss any suggestions that your partner has for revision and editing. Use the Revising Checklist on page 75 and the Editing Checklist on page 56. Write or type a revised version of your essay.

WRITING MORE PROBLEM/SOLUTION ESSAYS

Follow these steps to write another problem/solution essay.

Prewriting

A. Choose one of the following topics and freewrite about it for 10 minutes. Use a separate piece of paper if you do not have enough room here.

- Overcrowding in your school
- The generation gap
- An argument with a friend
- Smog
- Access to the workplace for the disabled

B. Using your freewriting as a basis for planning your essay, identify several of the solutions that you think you can develop into an essay. If you have not generated enough ideas, do another, more focused freewriting. Then prepare an outline of your essay.

READY TO WRITE

Writing

On a separate piece of paper, write the first draft of your essay. Use the essay plan on page 135 to help you with your draft. Be sure to provide some background information on the problem in the introduction and include a clear thesis statement. Organize the supporting paragraphs according to order of importance, beginning or ending with the most important solution. End with a conclusion that summarizes the solutions, draws a conclusion, or makes a prediction.

Revising and Editing

A. Personal revising. Wait at least one day, and then revise your essay using the checklist on page 75. Be sure that each paragraph describes one possible solution. Also, check to make sure you have provided enough support to explain each solution fully. Write or type a revised version of your essay.

B. Peer Revising. Exchange drafts with a classmate. Use the following worksheet as a guide for suggesting improvements in your partner's essay.

Writer: _____ Peer Editor: _____

1. What are some interesting things you learned from reading this essay? _____

   _____

   _____

2. Did the introduction provide enough background   _____ yes _____ no
   information to explain the problem?

3. How many solutions did the author offer in the essay?

   _____

   Is each solution adequately developed in a separate   _____ yes _____ no
   supporting paragraph?

4. Are the paragraphs arranged in a logical order?   _____ yes _____ no

   What type of order did the author use? _____

5. Did the author use transitions to guide you from   _____ yes _____ no
   one idea to the next?

6. Were there any irrelevant sentences that should   _____ yes _____ no
   be eliminated?

7. Did the author include a conclusion that   _____ yes _____ no
   summarizes the solutions or makes a prediction?

Incorporate any suggestions your classmate has made that you agree with.

C. Editing. Use the checklist on page 56 to edit your essay. Correct all the grammar, punctuation, capitalization, and spelling errors before you copy it over or type it.

Explore the Web

Think of a problem you might have in your everyday life: You spilled coffee on your carpet, you need directions to a nearby hospital, you want to buy an out-of-print book, you have a flat tire. Explore the Web to find a solution to your problem. Write a paragraph that describes the problem and explains the solution.

You Be the Editor

The following paragraph contains seven mistakes. Find the mistakes and correct them. Then copy the corrected paragraph onto a separate sheet of paper.

If you are like most people, you average one to three colds per year. Even if you do not have a cold right now. The chances are three in four that within the next year, at least one cold virus will find you. then you'll spend a week or so suffering from the miseries of the common cold: fatigue, sore throat, laryngitis, sneezing, stuffy or runny nose, and coughing. According to researchers, colds are the most common medical reason for missing school and work. Once you catch a cold, what can you do. There is no known cure yet for a cold. There are, however, several thing you can do to suppress the symptom's so that you feel better while the virus runs its course. For example, make sure that you get plenty of sleep and drink lots of liquids. You may find commercially available cold remedies such as decongestants, cough suppressants, and expectorants helpful, but keep in mind that these products can cause side effects. Many people prefer home remedies such as chicken soup, garlic, and ginger tea. In treating a cold, remember the wisdom of the ages, "if you treat a cold, it will be gone in a week; if you don't treat it, will be gone in seven days."

Source: *Jane Brody's Cold and Flu Fighter*

On Your Own

Write a problem/solution essay based on one of the problems you analyzed in the Brainstorming Solutions on pages 129–131. Be sure your essay has an introduction that describes the problem, several supporting paragraphs that explain the solutions, and a conclusion that summarizes the solutions or makes a prediction.

WRITING FOR SPECIFIC PURPOSES

In Part 1 of this book, you concentrated on the building blocks of good writing: prewriting and planning, developing a paragraph, organizing an essay, and revising and editing. Part 2 focused on the basics of the classic five-paragraph essays of process, division and classification, causes and effects, comparison/contrast, and problem/solution. In Part 3, you will turn your attention to the kinds of writing required for specific purposes such as writing summaries, expressing your opinions, and writing essays for undergraduate and graduate school applications. As you continue on the road to good writing, you will appreciate more and more the importance of matching your writing to your specific purpose.

CHAPTER 10

Writing Summaries

Preparing a summary requires a special kind of writing. Unlike the other types of writing you have done in this book, a summary should not include any of your own personal ideas. The only purpose of a summary is to condense what another author has written. This means reducing what the author has said to its main points.

Summaries are used in academic writing for every field. For example, in a business class, you might be asked to summarize an article from the *Wall Street Journal*. In a chemistry or physics class, a summary format is often used to prepare lab reports. In a literature class, you might be required to write summaries of novels or short stories.

Summarizing an Article

A good summary should present a clear, concise idea of the main points of an article to someone who has not read it. In order to write an effective summary, you need to have a true understanding of the original article. This means taking the time to read the article carefully to determine the author's purpose, main idea, and supporting points.

HOW TO WRITE A ONE-PARAGRAPH SUMMARY

The steps below will help you write an effective summary.

1. Read the article once to determine the author's thesis.
2. Reread the article and take notes on the main points.
3. Using your notes as a guide, write the first draft of your summary. It should include:
   a. A topic sentence that states the name of the article, (including the author, if available) and the main point.
   b. Supporting sentences that explain, in your own words, the main ideas presented in the article. An effective way to do this is by answering the questions *what, where, when, who,* and *why*.
   c. A final statement that summarizes any conclusions the author made in the article.

4. Revise the draft of your summary. Check to see that you have accurately summarized the author's main ideas. If you included any of the author's minor points, eliminate them. In addition, be sure that you did not include any of your own thoughts or opinions about the topic.

5. Edit your summary to make sure that the grammar, spelling, punctuation, and capitalization are correct.

Analyzing a One-Paragraph Summary

Read the article below and complete the exercise that follows.

What Will Our Towns Look Like? (If We Take Care of Our Planet)

Fantastic inventions made daily life easier in the past century but often at the expense of our natural resources. Gas-powered cars got us everywhere in a flash, but they polluted our air. Electric heat and light made our homes warm and welcoming but also burned up limited coal and oil. Factories revolutionized the way we worked, but industrial waste trashed rivers, streams, and oceans.

Lifestyle changes on the horizon for the next 100 years may actually improve our planet's health. We can use cleaner energy and fewer chemicals while working, playing, and bringing up families in the towns of tomorrow. This is not an impossible dream. Most of the innovations listed below already exist or are being developed. If we put our minds to it, our towns can preserve the Earth's natural riches and still be lovely places to call home. Here's how things might be—if we make the environment a top concern.

New inventions will help us build clean, green places to live.

WORK/TRANSPORTATION More adults will work in their homes and keep in touch with co-workers through computers. Others will make a short trip to a nearby office park. A few will ride swift electric trains to the nearest city. Cars and trucks will run on clean, hydrogen-powered fuel cells. Most entertainment and stores will be close by, so we'll often travel on old-fashioned, Earth-friendly bicycles.

FOOD We'll grow fruits, grains, and vegetables close to home, whether in our gardens or on nearby organic farms. Since the farms will use natural forms of pest control, such as predatory insects, there will be far fewer chemicals in the food supply.

SHOPPING Even if online stores are here to stay, there will still be a mall. But it will be small, with sidewalks and bike racks instead of a giant parking lot. An airy place in which a flood of natural light will cut down on energy use, the mall will be one big recycling operation; when you're through using any product you buy there, the store will be required to take it back for recycling.

ENERGY Our power will come from sources cleaner than coal, oil, and gas. Some energy will flow from windmills, but much of it will be generated in our own homes. Rooftop solar panels will supply electricity to our appliances and to a basement fuel cell, which will produce hydrogen. When the sun is not shining, the cell will use the hydrogen to make electricity.

WASTE Plumbing lines will empty into enclosed marshes, where special plants, fish, snails, and bacteria will naturally purify wastewater. Clean water will flow back into streams and reservoirs. ▪

1. Here are four summaries of the article. Read the summaries and decide which one is the best.

Summary 1

"What Will Our Towns Look Like? (If We Take Care of Our Planet)" describes the kind of new inventions that will help us build cleaner, greener places to live in the future. The author believes that if we work hard, we can build comfortable towns that maintain the Earth's natural riches at the same time.

Summary 2

This article is about how industries are trying to deal with the problem of environmental pollution in our towns. It's about time that we made the environment our top concern. Gas-powered cars, electric heat, and factories are not perfect solutions. We need to create new inventions in the future. If we want our towns to be clean and green, we need to make improvements in transportation, food, shopping, energy, and waste. I hope that in the not too distant future, many towns will be able to find the answer to the serious problem of pollution.

Summary 3

In "What Will Our Towns Look Like? (If We Take Care of Our Planet)," the author discusses new inventions that will help us build cleaner, more environmentally-friendly places to live. The author describes several lifestyle changes that might accomplish this goal within the next 100 years and predicts how things might be in the future if we are committed to protecting the environment. Specifically, the article mentions five areas that could be affected: work/transportation, food, shopping, energy, and waste. The predictions in each area show how it will be possible to build and live in comfortable towns that still maintain Earth's natural riches.

Summary 4

The article "What Will Our Planet Look Like?" talks about the ways we will live in the future. According to the article, gas-powered cars and trucks have added to the high level of pollution in the air we breathe. The author thinks that in the future cars and trucks will run on clean, hydrogen-powered fuel cells and our houses will be powered by windmills and solar energy. There will be rooftop solar panels on our houses to supply electicity to our appliances and to a basement fuel cell that produces hydrogen. We will eat safer food with no chemicals, drink cleaner water, and shop at stores that will be required to take products back for recycling. I think this article had a lot of good ideas about how to make the environment a top concern.

Which of the four summaries is the best? Why?

_____

_____

2. Analyze the other three summaries and determine what kinds of mistakes the authors made. Write the summary number and briefly describe the mistakes.

Summary: _____

Mistakes: _____

_____

_____

Summary: _____

Mistakes: _____

_____

_____

Summary: _____

Mistakes: _____

_____

_____

Completing a One-Paragraph Summary

Pretend you are doing research on planets outside our solar system that may support life. You found the following newspaper article, which announced the discovery of a new planet a few years ago. Read the article "New Planet May Support Life" and complete the summary that follows.

NEW PLANET MAY SUPPORT LIFE

by David L. Chandler

San Antonio—Astronomers announced to stunned colleagues yesterday the first discovery of a planet outside the solar system that may be capable of supporting life.

The find brings humankind to "a gateway to a new era in science," said Geoffrey W. Marcy, an astronomer at San Francisco State University and one of the two scientists who reported finding the planet. We now know, he said, that the Earth "has cousins in other solar systems. . . . Planets aren't rare, after all."

The discovery of the planet, in the constellation Virgo, culminates centuries of speculation and years of searching that produced a few intriguing results but never any sign of a planet resembling those in the solar system.

The planet, more than six times the size of Jupiter, orbits a star called 70 Virginis, which is almost a twin of the sun. And the planet's distance from that star—less than half the Earth's distance from the sun—suggests that it is likely to have a surface temperature of about 185 degrees Fahrenheit. That means that liquid water, the basis of all life as we know it, could exist there.

The find was one of two, and possibly three, planets outside the solar system whose discoveries were reported here yesterday at a meeting of the American Astronomical Society. The first confirmed sighting of a planet outside the solar system was announced by a Swiss team only three months ago.

"The exciting thing is that we found a planet where water could exist," said NASA administrator Daniel Goldin, who has made searching for other planets and indications of possible life elsewhere a top priority for the space agency. "On Earth, wherever we find water, we find life."

Robert Brown, an astronomer at the Space Telescope Science Institute and a specialist in planet formation, said, "What we are seeing here is the culmination of 500 years of intellectual history" that began when Copernicus found that the Earth was not the center of the universe.

Boston Globe, January 18, 1996

In "New Planet May Support Life" (*Boston Globe*, January 18, 1996),

_____ reports the first discovery made by

astronomers of _____ that might be able to support

life. This planet _____. Because the planet

probably has a surface temperature of _____,

experts believe it could _____. Scientists are very

excited about this discovery because _____.

Writing a One-Paragraph Summary

Complete the following steps to write a one-paragraph summary of "A Chimp Off the Old Block."

Prewriting

A. Read the article "A Chimp Off the Old Block" once to determine the main idea.

A Chimp Off the Old Block
by Curtis Rist

The chimp prodigy Ayumu demonstrates his literary skills by matching Japanese characters to colored shapes on a computer screen. Ai, a 25-year-old chimpanzee, is something of a celebrity due to her mental prowess. At the Kyoto University Primate Research Institute in Japan, she has learned to read several dozen characters in *kanji*, a form of written Japanese. Still, researchers were taken aback in February when they discovered that Ai's young son, Ayumu, may be teaching himself how to read.

Ai spends part of each day at a computer monitor, where she likes to match written words to colors and shapes so that she can earn 100-yen coins to buy snacks. On February 16, when only a video camera was watching, 10-month-old Ayumu jumped up to the monitor and correctly matched the kanji word for brown with a brown square. "It was astonishing," says Tetsuro Matsuzawa, a primatologist at the institute. "He had never even touched the screen before." Researchers are now hopeful that Ayumu will continue to learn simply by observing his mother, without having to be coached.

So what did the precocious primate do with the 100 yen earned for making his first word match? "He bought some raisins from our vending machine," says Matsuzawa. "They're his favorite."

Discover magazine, January 2002
Photograph by Tony Law

B. Write the main idea.

_____

_____

C. Read the article again and take notes on the important points.

Write a first draft of your summary. Include only the main points of the article. Try to answer the questions *what, where, when, who,* and *why.*

READY TO WRITE

_____

_____

_____

_____

_____

_____

Revising and Editing

A. Peer Revising. Exchange papers with a partner. Use the following worksheet as a guide for suggesting improvements in your partner's summary.

> Writer: _____ Peer Editor: _____
>
> 1. Does the summary begin with a sentence that states the name and main idea of the article? _____ yes _____ no
>
> 2. Does the summary present the main supporting points? _____ yes _____ no
>
> 3. Was the writer careful not to include any minor details or personal opinions? _____ yes _____ no
>
> 4. Does the summary end with a statement that summarizes the author's conclusion? _____ yes _____ no

Incorporate any suggestions your classmate has made that you agree with.

B. Personal Revising. Revise your essay using the checklist on page 75. Write or type a revised version of your essay.

C. Editing. Use the checklist on page 56 to edit your summary. Correct all the grammar, punctuation, capitalization, and spelling errors before you copy it over or type it.

A. Read the following article about Franklin Delano Roosevelt and the disease that handicapped him eleven years before he was elected president of the United States in 1932.

POLITICS AS USUAL

by Diana Childress

When polio paralyzed Franklin Roosevelt in August 1921, he put on a brave front. Having learned from childhood to bear pain "without fuss," he joked about a thirty-nine-year-old man getting a baby's disease and radiated optimism about his recovery. "The doctors say," he wrote a friend in December, "that by this Spring I will be walking without any limp."

But as Franklin's wife, Eleanor, said later, "I know that he had real fear when he was first taken ill." Polio was "a trial by fire." A big question in everyone's mind was how this crippling blow would affect Franklin's future in politics.

For Sara Roosevelt, the answer was perfectly clear. Her son, she felt, had already served his country well. With her money to support him, he could retire to the family home in Hyde Park and enjoy his business interests and hobbies.

Sara's views were typical of the times. In the early 1900s, people with physical disabilities were treated like invalids, either hospitalized or kept at home. Many thought it "bad manners" for a disabled person to appear in public. The idea of a "cripple" pursuing a political career was unthinkable.

Eleanor also doubted that her husband could ever return to public office. But she knew how important Franklin's political ambitions were to him. The doctors told her that keeping hope alive would improve his chances of recovery. Taking an active part in life, even if it tired him, was "better for his condition," they said. So she encouraged and helped him to stay involved in politics.

Louis Howe, Franklin's longtime political adviser, added his support. Within days after falling ill, Franklin was dictating letters that he could not even sign because the paralysis had temporarily spread to his arms and thumbs. He agreed to become a member of the executive committee of the Democratic party in New York State even though at that time, as one biographer notes, he was lying in bed and "working for hours to try to wiggle a big toe."

With Howe's help, Franklin kept the general public from finding out how seriously ill he was. Meanwhile, he worked feverishly to try to regain the use of his legs. Determined to make a full recovery, he spent much of his time exercising and struggling to learn to walk. When Democratic leaders urged him to run for U.S. senator or governor of New York in 1922, he had to admit he was not ready. Yet he kept busy on the sidelines, writing letters and articles while Howe and Eleanor appeared for him in public.

In 1924, Franklin could not avoid the Democratic National Convention and still be taken seriously as a politician. The agile man who had vaulted over a row of chairs to reach the speaker's platform in 1920 now inched painfully forward on crutches. "But nothing was the matter with his voice or his enthusiasm," wrote a reporter. His half-hour speech nominating Al Smith for president was cheered for one hour thirteen minutes.

Four years later, Franklin still hoped that another year or two of rehabilitation would free him from his wheelchair and crutches. He tried to avoid the calls from the New York State Democratic Convention urging him to accept the nomination for governor. But when the Democratic presidential candidate, Al Smith, finally got him on the line, he realized he could no longer plead illness without letting his party down.

Franklin Roosevelt's return to active politics in spite of his inability to walk was a major triumph for himself and for disabled people everywhere. He never achieved full recovery, but his years of hard work brought a maturity and a depth of understanding that enhanced his greatness as a leader. ∎

Source: *Cobblestone*

Reread the article and take notes in the space below on the important points. On a separate piece of paper, write a one-paragraph summary based on your notes. Remember to revise and edit your summary before you hand it in.

**READY
TO WRITE**

_____

_____

_____

_____

_____

B. Read the following newspaper article that was written when hockey star Wayne Gretzky retired from playing professional ice hockey. Then on a separate piece of paper, summarize the article in one paragraph.

WAYNE GRETZKY: A HOCKEY HERO

by Daniel Lourie

Every sport has its legends, those few players who truly make the game magical. For the sport of ice hockey, that legend is Canadian-born skater John Wayne Gretzky. It is fitting that he is referred to as "The Great One" by fans all over the world. Last night "The Great One" announced his retirement at a news conference in Madison Square Garden. "Whether it's now or next year or 20 years from now, I'll always miss and always love hockey," he said. His fans say, "Whether it's now or next year or 20 years from now, we'll always miss and always love you."

Not only is Wayne Gretzky the best player of his generation, he is probably the best ice hockey player of all time. Of course, such a title does not come without accomplishments, and Gretzky certainly has his share of success stories. His incredible skill as a player is well documented. For one thing, he has scored more goals and points than any player in pro hockey history. In addition, Gretzky has set over sixty world records. He won eight consecutive Hart Trophies as the league's Most Valuable Player, and seven consecutive Art Ross Trophies, awarded to the NHL's top scorer. Since he began playing at the age of three, Gretzky's passion for ice hockey has never waned.

Wayne Gretzky, however, is not just an amazing athlete; it takes much more than athletic skill to earn the title of best player of all time. Gretzky also displayed remarkable sportsmanship, both on and off the ice. This quality won him praise and admiration from all sporting arenas. In fact, Gretzky won the NHL's award for sportsmanship five times. He is truly a team player whose ability to improve the performances of his teammates is well known.

Certainly this combination of athletic skill and sportsmanship is enough to make any athlete famous. But it is Wayne's charisma and charm that has made him revered. Throughout his career, Gretzky has always impressed his peers by capturing the hearts of million of fans with his warm, down-to-earth manner.

For all of the above reasons, it is not difficult to imagine how Gretzky has earned himself millions of incredibly loyal fans. In his country of origin, Canada, Gretzky is a national hero. So, it really should be no surprise that when Gretzky decided to retire from the sport that made him famous, an entire nation was saddened.

Although Wayne Gretzky may be retiring, his legend will not be forgotten. The record-breaking player will be immortalized not only through the memory of his fans, but also by a recently released song entitled "Number 99" (Gretzky's jersey number). Written by Canadian singer Cheryl Lescom, the song is a lasting tribute to the man who changed the face of ice hockey. "Number 99" commemorates Gretzky's achievements in the game and the example he set for young people in Canada. Money raised from CD sales of the song will be donated to Canadian youth hockey programs. In the end, a song such as "Number 99" is a perfect way to honor such a legendary hero, for it is a lasting tribute to a man who gave so much to his sport, to his fans, and to his country.

Explore the Web

Many newspapers and magazines are on-line. Choose a topic in the news that you are interested in. It can be a local story, a national story, or an international story. Explore the Web to find several articles on the topic. Read the articles, and choose the one that is the most interesting or informative. Print out the article, read it again carefully, and write a one-paragraph summary of it.

You Be the Editor

The following paragraph is a summary of a magazine article. The content of the summary is correct, but there are eight mistakes. Find the mistakes and correct them. Then copy the corrected paragraph on a separate piece of paper.

> In the article "The Growing of Green cars," W. E. Butterworth discusses the new trends in environmentally safe automobiles called "green cars." Automakers are working hardly to produce cars that cause less pollution. They're long-term goal is to make zero-emission vehicles (ZEV) to comply with new state laws. The author mentions several way that car companies can reach their goal, such as designing cars that burn less fuel, tuning engines so they burn more cleaner fuels, and producing electric cars that do not burn any fuel. However, each one of these solutions has a drawback, and many of them is expensive. Although everyone agree that there are no simple solutions. More and more states are adopting stricter antipollution laws.

On Your Own

Choose a newspaper or magazine article on any topic that interests you. Read it carefully, and on a separate piece of paper, write a one-paragraph summary of it. Bring the article and your summary to class to share with your classmates.

CHAPTER 11

Expressing Your Opinions

As a writer, you might be asked to give your opinion of a controversial topic in the news. You might also be asked to express your opinion about something you have read, seen, or heard.

Opinion papers have a very important place in academic writing. In some classes you will be required to give your opinion of a topic you have discussed or an article or a book you have read. For example, in a literature class, a professor might ask for your reaction to a poem or short story. In a music class, an assignment could involve writing a reaction to a piece of music.

Expressing Your Opinion about Controversial Issues

Issue 1

Prewriting

A. Read the following newspaper article about two convicted murderers who were put to death for crimes they had been convicted of committing many years before.

What Is Justice?

TWO MEN WERE PUT TO DEATH last week in the United States for murders that they had been convicted of committing many years ago. Billy Bailey died in the first hanging in Delaware in fifty years. It was twenty years ago that he murdered an elderly couple after breaking into their home. John Taylor, a child rapist and murderer, was shot by a five-man firing squad in Utah.

Polls show that about 70 percent of U.S. citizens favor capital punishment. Many believe that people who commit horrendous crimes deserve to die brutally in return for the brutality that they inflicted on their victims: Others protest the barbarism of the death penalty, be it by lethal injection, electric chair, firing squad, or hanging. While there were many people who supported the two deaths that took place last week, there were also many protesters.

B. In small groups discuss the article and answer the following questions.

    a. What is your opinion about capital punishment? Do you think there are any situations where it is an appropriate method of punishment?

    b. Do you think capital punishment helps prevent crime? Why or why not?

    c. Do you know of another country that uses capital punishment? Why does that country use it?

C. Brainstorm a list of reasons that support your opinion about capital punishment.

Writing

On a separate piece of paper, write a paragraph that expresses your opinion about the use of capital punishment in cases such as the two described in the article. Begin with a topic sentence that states the issue and your opinion. Organize your supporting sentences according to order of importance.

Revising and Editing

Exchange drafts with a classmate. Use the checklists on pages 56 and 75. Discuss any suggestions that your partner has for revision and editing. Write or type a revised version of your essay.

Issue 2

Prewriting

A. Choose one of the following topics and freewrite about it for ten minutes.

- Your opinion about the use of animals for laboratory experiments
- Your opinion about women serving in the military
- Your opinion about same-sex schools

B. Brainstorm a list of reasons, facts, or examples to support your opinion.

C. Use your freewriting and brainstorming as a basis for planning your paragraph.

Writing

On a separate piece of paper, write the first draft of your paragraph. Begin with a topic sentence that states the issue and your opinion about it. Organize the supporting sentences according to order of importance, beginning or ending with the most important reason. End with a concluding sentence that summarizes your opinion.

Revising and Editing

Exchange drafts with a classmate. Use the checklists on pages 56 and 75. Discuss any suggestions that your partner has for revision and editing. Write or type a revised version of your essay.

Pretend you are married to one of the managers of a small computer company in Toronto, Canada. Your spouse has just received the following memo. Read the memo and complete the exercise that follows.

MEMO

TO: All Employees
FROM: Jim Philips
RE: Merger with Logicom
DATE: June 30, 2_____

As most of you know, we have been talking for several months now with the people at Logicom about merging our two companies. We are pleased to announce that the details have been worked out and we will be combining our companies. The official merger date is set for October 5. We are confident that we can look forward to a long and successful alliance with Logicom, since our products complement each other so well. This merger should lead to greater success in the marketplace than either company could achieve on its own.

This memo is also to confirm that as per Logicom's insistence, we will be moving our offices and people to Montreal. We know that this will be difficult and disruptive for some of you, but we sincerely believe that it is in the best interests of the company. We hope that each and every one of you will join us in this exciting opportunity. Further details regarding the merger and the move will be sent to you shortly.

Writing

Write a letter to your parents or a close friend that expresses your opinion about this news.

Dear _____,

Love,

_____

Revise, edit, and copy your letter over before handing it in.

Expressing Your Opinion about a Piece of Art

Painting 1

Look at the painting by Jackson Pollock called *Number 10.* Then read one student's opinion about it.

The first time I saw a Jackson Pollock painting in a museum, I just kept walking because I didn't find it interesting. It seemed too abstract to me, too untraditional, and incomprehensible. I wasn't even tempted to stop and read the label. The second time I saw it, I stopped to read the label. I learned that the painting was called *Number 10* and that Pollock put the canvas on the floor and moved around it, pouring and dripping paint from a large brush with big, bold sweeping movements of his arm. He used industrial enamel paint, the kind used on automobiles. The more I looked at the painting, the more I began to appreciate it. I appreciated that he had an unconventional way of painting and that he was freely expressing himself. I began to realize that there is no real subject to his paintings—the physical act of painting is the subject. I realized that I can decide for myself what I see in his paintings but that I must not ascribe my ideas to him. I also loved that when asked about the meaning of his work he responded, "When you see a flower bed do you tear your hair out looking for meaning?"

Discuss the Jackson Pollock painting and the student's opinion of it with a partner. What is your opinion of the painting? What is the student's opinion?

Painting 2

Look at the painting by John Singleton Copley called *Watson and the Shark.* Then read the information about the artist and the painting.

John Singleton Copley was one of the most important North American painters of the eighteenth century. He painted huge and dramatic paintings based on important events of his time. His paintings were often very realistic.

Watson and the Shark is one of Copley's most memorable works. It tells the true story of a man named Watson who was attacked by a shark while he was swimming in Havana Harbor. Watson was dramatically rescued and asked Copley to paint a picture of his story. Copley made the painting as realistic as he could. Some art historians think that the shark symbolizes evil and that the man rescuing Watson symbolizes good. They believe that Watson himself symbolizes the way we all struggle between the forces of good and evil.

Prewriting

Discuss the painting with a partner and answer the following questions.

1. What do you see when you look at the painting? Describe the people and their surroundings. You may need to use your dictionary.
2. What is happening in the painting?
3. How does the painting make you feel? Do you like the painting? Why or why not?
4. How does the painting symbolize the conflict between good and evil?

READY TO WRITE

Writing

On a separate piece of paper, write a paragraph describing your opinion of *Watson and the Shark.*

Revising and Editing

Exchange drafts with a partner. Use the checklists on pages 56 and 75. Discuss any suggestions that your partner has for revision and editing. Write or type a revised version of your essay.

Painting 3

Look at the painting by Andrew Wyeth. Then read the information about the artist and the painting.

Andrew Wyeth is another important North American painter. He is known for his realistic interpretations of people and landscapes, his technical brilliance, and his affection for his subjects. He found inspiration in his everyday surroundings. One of Wyeth's best-known paintings is called *Christina's World*.

Prewriting

Discuss your impressions of the painting with a partner and answer the questions below.

1. What do you see when you look at the painting? Describe the woman and her surroundings. You may need to use your dictionary.
2. What seems to be happening in the painting?
3. What story do you think the artist is trying to tell?
4. What adjectives would you use to describe the painting?

Writing

On a separate piece of paper, write your opinion of *Christina's World*.

Revising and Editing

Exchange drafts with a classmate. Use the checklists on pages 56 and 75. Discuss any suggestions that your partner has for revision and editing. Write or type a revised version of your essay.

READY TO WRITE

Follow-up Activity

Christina's World depicts one of Wyeth's neighbors, a woman named Christina, who was paralyzed. Wyeth's belief that life contains hardship and suffering is reflected by Christina, who stretches awkwardly toward the farmhouse that is beyond her ability to reach. Art experts point out the mood of despair and the sense of frustration in the painting. They think this painting is about life's limitations and unattainable goals.

Look at the painting again, now that you know the story behind it. Answer the following questions.

1. What aspects of the painting express a mood of despair and a sense of frustration?

_____

_____

2. Do you see that the painting is about life's limitations and unattainable goals? Why or why not?

_____

_____

_____

3. What is your opinion of the painting now that you know the story that Wyeth was trying to tell? Write a paragraph explaining your new response.

_____

_____

_____

_____

_____

_____

_____

Expressing Your Opinion about a Photograph

Prewriting

A. Look at the two photos.

B. Answer the following questions.

1. Describe what is happening in each photo.
2. Which photo do you like better? Why?
3. Which photo has more meaning for you? Why?
4. Which photo would you find it easier to write about?

Writing

On a separate piece of paper, write your opinion about one of the photos.

Revising and Editing

Exchange drafts with someone who chose the same photo you did. Compare and contrast your opinions. Then help each other revise and edit using the checklists on pages 56 and 75. Write or type a revised version of your essay.

Responding to Quotations

Many writing assignments involve responding to quotations. You might be asked to explain the meaning of a quotation and then give your opinion of it.

A. Read the following quotations from around the world and put a checkmark next to those that you find especially interesting. In small groups, discuss the quotes that all the members of your group checked.

_____ 1. Patience is power. (Chinese proverb)

_____ 2. The main thing in one's own private world is to try to laugh as much as you cry. (Maya Angelou)

_____ 3. It is very tiring to hate. (Jean Rostand)

_____ 4. Anyone who looks for a perfect friend will remain without friends. (Turkish proverb)

_____ 5. We are shaped by what we love. (Johann Wolfgang von Goethe)

_____ 6. Jealousy is a tiger that tears not only its prey but also its own raging heart. (Michael Beer)

_____ 7. Happiness sneaks in through a door you didn't know you left open. (John Barrymore)

_____ 8. Life shrinks or expands according to one's courage. (Anaïs Nin)

_____ 9. Humility is the root, mother, nurse, foundation, and bond of all virtue. (St. John Chrysostom)

_____ 10. Winning is neither everything nor the only thing; it is one of many things. (Joan Benoit Samuelson)

_____ 11. A human life is like a letter of the alphabet. It can be meaningless. Or it can be part of a great meaning. (Anonymous)

_____ 12. I hate television. I hate it as much as I hate peanuts. But I can't stop eating peanuts. (Orson Welles)

B. Choose one of the quotes you discussed with your group and write a one-paragraph response to it. Be sure to include the quote at the beginning of your paragraph. Explain why you chose that quote and how it has meaning for you.

C. Read your reactions to the other members of your group for their feedback. Then revise, edit, and copy your response over before handing it in.

Expressing Your Opinion about a Poem

A.   Read the information about Robert Frost and his poem "The Road Not Taken."

Robert Frost (1874–1963) is one of the most important North American poets of the twentieth century. "The Road Not Taken" tells the story of an important choice the author made in his life.

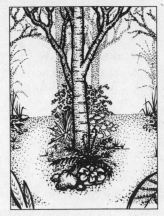

The Road Not Taken

I.   Two roads diverged in a yellow wood,[1]
     And sorry I could not travel both
     And be one traveler, long I stood
     And looked down one as far as I could
     To where it bent in the undergrowth;[2]

II. Then took the other, as just as fair,[3]
     And having perhaps the better claim,
     Because it was grassy and wanted wear;[4]
     Though as for that the passing there
     Had worn them really about the same,

III. And both that morning equally lay
     In leaves no step had trodden black.[5]
     Oh, I kept the first for another day!
     Yet knowing how way leads on to way,[6]
     I doubted if I should ever come back.

IV. I shall be telling this with a sigh
     Somewhere ages and ages hence:[7]
     Two roads diverged in a wood, and I—
     I took the one less traveled by,
     And that has made all the difference.

—Robert Frost

[1] One road divided into two roads in a forest
[2] To the place where it turned under the low bushes
[3] I took the other road, which was just as nice
[4] Because it was slightly overgrown and less used
[5] No one had walked on either road yet that day
[6] I knew how one road often leads to another road
[7] In some place in the future

Prewriting

The four stanzas (groups of lines) of the poem each tell a part of the story. Read each stanza again and think about what it means. Then look at the following summaries. Each summary refers to one of the stanzas in the poem. Match each summary with the stanza it refers to.

1. He decided to take the road that looked like it had not been used as much.

    Stanza _____

2. Sometime in the future, he will remember this day when he had to make a choice and be glad that he took the road that was less traveled.

    Stanza _____

3. A man was walking in the woods and he came to a place where the single road divided into two separate roads. He was sorry that he could not take both roads.

   Stanza _____

4. Although he chose the second road, he hoped that he would be able to return some day to take the first one. But he doubted that he ever would.

   Stanza _____

Writing

Robert Frost's poem is based on a choice he had to make. Think about an important choice that you have made. On a separate piece of paper, describe the situation and the effect your choice has had on your life.

READY TO WRITE

Revising and Editing

Exchange drafts with a classmate. Use the checklists on pages 56 and 75. Discuss any suggestions that your partner has for revision and editing. Write or type a revised version of your essay.

B. Read the information about Emily Dickinson and her poem "Hope Is the Thing with Feathers."

Emily Dickinson (1830–1886) is another of North America's gifted poets. "Hope Is the Thing with Feathers" is one of Dickinson's most famous poems. In this poem, she uses the metaphor of a bird to describe her feelings about hope.

Prewriting

Hope Is the Thing with Feathers

Hope is the thing with feathers
That perches[1] in the soul,
And sings the tune without the words,
And never stops at all.

And sweetest in the gale[2] is heard;
And sore must be the storm
That could abash[3] the little bird
That kept so many warm.

I've heard it in the chillest land,
And on the strangest sea;
Yet, never, in extremity[4],
It asked a crumb[5] of me.

—Emily Dickinson

[1] sits
[2] strong wind
[3] upset
[4] an extreme situation
[5] a small piece of food

Discuss your opinion of the poem with a partner.

**READY
TO WRITE**

Writing

Emily Dickinson describes hope as a thing with feathers. How would you describe hope? Write a paragraph about one of the following topics.

1. A time in your life when hope was very important
2. Your hopes for the future
3. Your own description of hope

Revising and Editing

Exchange drafts with a classmate. Use the checklists on pages 56 and 75. Discuss any suggestions that your partner has for revision and editing. Write or type a revised version of your essay.

Metaphor Activity

A metaphor is a phrase that describes something by comparing it to something else without the words *like* or *as.* Reread the first two lines of Emily Dickinson's poem. Using these lines as a model, create your own metaphors for each of the following words.

Example

Happiness is a <u>flower</u> with <u>buds</u> that <u>blossoms in my heart.</u>

1. Jealousy is a/an _____ with _____
   that _____

2. Beauty is a/an _____ with _____
   that _____

3. Hate is a/an _____ with _____
   that _____

4. Love is a/an _____ with _____
   that _____

5. Wisdom is a/an _____ with _____
   that _____

6. Fear is a/an _____ with _____
   that _____

Explore the Web

The Internet has many lists of famous sayings or pieces of advice. Explore the Web to find some of these lists. Write down five interesting sayings or pieces of advice and share them with your classmates. Choose one and write a paragraph explaining your own opinion of the saying or the piece of advice.

You Be the Editor

The following e-mail contains seven mistakes. Find the mistakes and correct them. Then copy the corrected message onto a separate piece of paper.

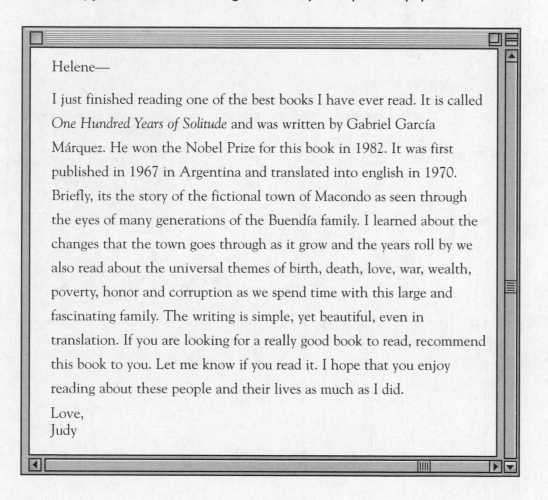

Helene—

I just finished reading one of the best books I have ever read. It is called *One Hundred Years of Solitude* and was written by Gabriel García Márquez. He won the Nobel Prize for this book in 1982. It was first published in 1967 in Argentina and translated into english in 1970. Briefly, its the story of the fictional town of Macondo as seen through the eyes of many generations of the Buendía family. I learned about the changes that the town goes through as it grow and the years roll by we also read about the universal themes of birth, death, love, war, wealth, poverty, honor and corruption as we spend time with this large and fascinating family. The writing is simple, yet beautiful, even in translation. If you are looking for a really good book to read, recommend this book to you. Let me know if you read it. I hope that you enjoy reading about these people and their lives as much as I did.

Love,
Judy

On Your Own

A. Look at the two cartoons below. Choose one and write your reaction to the ideas expressed in the cartoon.

Drawing by Rini, © 1995 *The New Yorker* Magazine, Inc.

B. Write your opinion about a song, TV program, or movie. You may choose one that you are familiar with or one that you have just seen or heard for the first time.

CHAPTER 12

Writing Essays for Undergraduate and Graduate School Applications

If you are planning to apply to undergraduate or graduate school in the United States, you will probably have to write a personal essay as part of the application process. Some schools will give you very structured questions, and others will give you more open-ended questions. In this chapter, you will practice writing answers to typical application essay questions.

Tips for Writing Application Essays

1. **Take the essay part of the application very seriously.** To some schools, the essay is the most important part of your application. Admissions officers at more than one school have said that the essay can make or break a candidate's chances for admission.

2. **Be honest. Be yourself. Be sincere.** The admissions committees want to know who you are as a person. Do not misrepresent yourself.

3. **Write about something that is important to you.** Even if you are given a specific subject to write about, you will have to choose your angle. Let your enthusiasm for the subject show. Your interest in the subject is a very important, sometimes the most important, element in an essay.

4. **Make your application as interesting and lively as you can.** Admissions officers read hundreds, maybe thousands, of essays. You want yours to stand out.

(continues)

5. **Do not try to write the application essay in a hurry or at the last minute.** You need to give yourself time to think about the question and do some prewriting and planning before you actually write the essay.

6. **Keep your audience and your purpose in mind as you plan and write your essay.**

7. **Pay attention to the principles of good writing that you have studied in this book.** Make sure you have a main idea, support, and clear organization. Include specific details so that your essay is uniquely about you. Do not write an essay that is so general that it could have been written by any number of other people. Add details to bring your essay to life.

8. **Follow the rules you have learned in this book for writing a good introduction, body, and conclusion.**

9. **Your essay must be as perfect as you can make it.** This means no grammatical, spelling, punctuation, or capitalization mistakes. Have several people—teachers, relatives, and/or friends—read it carefully for you. Remember that neatness counts.

10. **Make a copy of your essay before you mail it.** This will avoid problems if your application gets lost in the mail or in the admissions office. To be safe, send it registered mail with a return receipt requested.

Whether you are applying to undergraduate or graduate school, there are several principles that you should pay attention to in writing your essay. Even if you are not planning to attend a university in the United States, you will improve your writing skills by practicing this kind of essay.

Undergraduate Essays

The application essay is very important to admissions committees. They use it to get to know the individual behind the test scores and grade point average. You should think of your essay as a chance to show yourself off to your best advantage. Try to tell them a little more about yourself than they would know by reading the rest of your application. Admissions committees also use the essay to determine how well you write because good writing skills are important for success in college. In short, your essay is your special opportunity to prove that you are an interesting person and that you can write well.

Analyzing an Undergraduate Essay

Here is an example of an essay that was written in response to a university's request:

In reading your application, we want to get to know you as well as we can. We ask that you use this opportunity to tell us something more about yourself that would help us toward a sense of who you are, how you think, and what issues and ideas interest you the most.

Read the essay and answer the questions that follow.

Scuba diving has never been easy for me. When I was in fifth grade, the father of one of my classmates died in a scuba-diving accident. His death, along with the scenes I had watched in James Bond movies of men left to drown hundreds of feet under water with severed air tubes, did not give me the impression that scuba diving was a safe sport. However, in eighth grade, my father asked me if I would take scuba-diving classes with him. Although I was reluctant, the important fact was that he would be there to support me and that we would do it together. It seemed that as I grew older, we spent less time together. I wanted this opportunity to be with him.

After hours of pool work and classes, I was ready to go for my certification. My first problem was getting to the dive site. I have a slight fear of boats, which probably stems from my first boat ride, during which I developed a major case of seasickness. This was a small obstacle compared to what was about to come. I spent the first fifteen minutes of the dive standing on the rocking deck of the dive boat, staring at the rough ocean, weak with fear. I was only able to dive into the water after a good pep talk from both my father and my dive master. I repeated the word "relax" to myself over and over and plunged in.

Even now, after five years of scuba diving, I still feel a little uneasy before submerging. However, once I have taken a deep breath and broken the surface of the water, curiosity and astonishment at the variety on the ocean floor calm my apprehensions. No sounds or disturbances break the perfect tranquility. Enormous purple fans wave in the current, and orange and red sponges jut out of the coral like poppies in a meadow. When I am underwater, I can hover above the colorful, craggy coral, flying like Superman, watching schools of fish dart around in search of food, oblivious to my presence. Underwater, I am able to leave behind my worries and observe the peaceful beauty of nature.

The experience does not end with my surfacing but continues with the stories my father, the other divers, and I tell afterward. There is a high level of camaraderie among all divers. We sit around like old pirates in a dank tavern, laughing as we talk about the stingrays who search for food in our hair (an experience that was once described as "like being mugged by E.T.") or about the dive master who found a bicycle down by one of the wrecks and started to ride it around. My fellow divers do not know that I have not yet left behind my fears of diving, because once I submerge, I inhabit a different world with them.

Like learning to scuba dive, learning to read was also not easy for me. Most early-reading programs rely heavily on the teaching of phonetics. However, I have a learning disability that makes understanding sound/symbol relationships difficult. This made learning to read through the use of phonetics impossible. I was lucky, though, because I was accepted into Fenn School's Intensive Language Program. For two years (fourth and fifth grades), six other boys and I worked together, learning how to compensate for our learning differences. In this class, I developed a trait that I am very proud of: the ability to work hard—not only in my studies, but in everything I do.

By continuing even when the waters were rough, and drawing on the support of my parents and teachers, I learned to read and found an amazing world opened to me. Just as my fellow divers do not know that I am anxious about scuba diving, most of my classmates do not know that I have a learning disability. They just think that I am a diligent worker, but I know that, as with scuba diving, there is a lot more to the story.

1. What two experiences did the student write about? How are they related? What was his purpose in talking about scuba diving?

   _____

   _____

   _____

2. What did you learn about this student? What adjectives would you use to describe him?

   _____

   _____

   _____

3. What does the essay reveal about the author's relationship with his father? His value system?

   _____

   _____

   _____

SAMPLE ESSAY QUESTIONS

The most common application essay is the one that asks you for autobiographical information. Some schools ask for it directly with questions such as, "Tell us a little about yourself" or "Give the admissions committee information about yourself that is not included elsewhere on the application." Other schools ask the question indirectly with such questions as, "What person has influenced you most in life?"

Here are some typical essay topics that are often used by colleges and universities in the United States. In small groups, discuss the topics and make notes about how you might answer each one.

1. Evaluate a significant experience or achievement that has special meaning to you.
2. Discuss some issue of personal, local, or national concern and its importance to you.
3. Indicate a person who has had a significant influence on you and describe that influence.
4. What one word best describes you and why?
5. If you could change any event in history, what would you change and why?
6. Describe the most difficult thing that you have ever done.
7. What book has affected you most and why?
8. Describe a change that you have gone through and how it may affect your future.

Writing an Essay for an Undergraduate Application

Prewriting

A. Choose three of the essay topics above and, on a separate piece of paper, freewrite about each one for ten minutes.

B. Reread your three freewriting samples and choose one of them to develop into an essay. Using the ideas you generated in your prewriting, prepare an outline of the essay.

Writing

On a separate piece of paper, write the first draft of your essay. Be sure to start with an interesting introduction that will make the admissions committee excited about reading your essay. You should choose a method of organization for your supporting paragraphs, such as time order or order of importance, that best suits your topic. Include specific details and examples that will help the committee get to know you. Finally, make your conclusion one that the readers will remember.

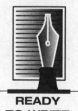

READY TO WRITE

Revising and Editing

A. Wait at least one day, and then revise your essay using the checklist on page 75. Write or type a revised version of your essay.

B. Use the checklist on page 56 to edit your essay. Correct all the grammar, punctuation, capitalization, and spelling errors. Give your essay to your teacher and someone else to read for any final comments before you copy it over or type it.

You Be the Editor

Most applications also include several short-answer questions. Do not be deceived by these questions. They are just as important as the longer essay questions, and the same principles apply.

Read the following student response to the short-answer question, "Tell us about the academic areas that interest you most." There are seven mistakes. Find and correct the mistakes.

> I am interested in mathematic and science, but at this point I have not yet identified a specific area to major in. I am also interest in learning more about the field of engineering. At Blake University I can to explore all of these areas, before I decide upon a major. Blake even offer the opportunity to combine them into an interdisciplinary major. finally, although I do not intend to major in art, I have a strong interest in art and find the possible of taking courses at Blake's School of Design attractive.

Filling Out an Application

Many colleges and universities in the United States use the same application form. It is called the *common application.* Turn to the appendix on pages 174–175 to see a sample common application from several years ago. Just for practice, take the time to fill it out completely. Make sure that your information is accurate and your handwriting neat and legible.

Graduate School Essays

The biggest difference between essays for undergraduate and graduate school is in the subject matter. A graduate school essay focuses on career goals and is generally referred to as a *statement of purpose.* The tips for writing application essays that you read on pages 165–166 are useful for both types of essays.

Analyzing a Graduate School Statement of Purpose

Here is an example of a successful graduate school statement of purpose. This student wants to study civil engineering at the University of Michigan.

Statement of Purpose: (Type or print clearly on a separate piece of paper.) Your statement of purpose should be a concise, well-written essay about your background, your career goals, and how Michigan's graduate program will help you meet your career and educational objectives.

Read the statement of purpose essay and answer the questions that follow.

My lifelong passion for structures and construction was sparked in 1978 when I got my first LEGO set. I would spend hours imagining and drawing buildings and bridges and trying to make them out of LEGO pieces. My father is a civil engineer, and one of my greatest joys was accompanying him to oversee the progress at his construction sites. Nothing was more intriguing to me then than watching a structure transform from a sketch on an engineer's pad to a building in our community. I can still remember the sense of pride I felt upon the completion of the dam my father had engineered. Ever since I was a child, my dream has been to become a civil engineer and join my father in his company. Over the years, my dream has not changed, but the path to my goal has become more complicated. As I watched Turkey go through a series of political and economic changes, I felt the great effect it had on companies like my father's. I came to realize that in order to be a successful civil engineer, I would need to acquire a diversity of skills.

When I was in high school, the Turkish economy was tightly held in the hands of the government. Almost all major industries were dominated by government monopolies, leaving little room for the private sector to flourish. Then, seemingly overnight, Turkey went from an economy based on small family businesses and government-held industries to a competitive market modeled on the Western style. The privatization of Turkish industries in the late 1980s and a concurrent influx of foreign investments led to the birth of big corporations in all industries, including construction. However, the transition has not always been a smooth one. Turkey lacked a solid core of educated business professionals capable of dealing with the rapid economic growth that involved newly defined business relations at corporate levels. There was only a handful of Turkish businesspeople skilled at negotiating with managers of foreign companies.

Realizing this need, I decided that the first step of my educational plan should be to study business and finance at a university in the United States. This would provide me with the solid foundation of knowledge and skills that I would need in my construction management career. When I left home to come to the United States, Turkey was on the brink of a new era. During the five years that I have been here completing my undergraduate education, Turkey has undergone tremendous changes in all spheres: political, social, economic, and technological. Old systems and traditional models were replaced with contemporary ones as Western influences became more dominant.

During the past five years, I have become fluent in English while earning a bachelor of science degree in finance, with a minor in economics. I am currently completing a second bachelor's degree in mathematics. Now, I will further my education by pursuing graduate studies in civil engineering. Turkey's recent economic boom has brought an unprecedented wave of unmanaged construction in urban areas, revealing a need for highly trained engineers with managerial skills. The Construction Engineering and Management program at the University of Michigan will expand upon my present management knowledge and train me in the engineering skills necessary to plan, coordinate, and control the diverse range of specialists involved in the construction industry. I feel that my background in economics and finance, coupled with my strong quantitative skills, makes me an excellent candidate for graduate studies in this field.

Michigan's Construction Engineering and Management program will prepare me for a responsible management position in the construction industry. At Michigan, I hope to be involved in research that investigates the applications of artificial intelligence techniques as well as computer applications in the construction industry. I would also like to research strategies for innovation in construction, especially as they relate to a developing country. Finally, I am interested in how the planning, design, and implementation of engineering projects are integrated into a coherent, well-functioning system. I hope to improve my understanding of the whole system by examining how the subsystems and various components fit together.

Since one of my goals is to improve the operation and management of Turkey's present inefficient infrastructure, I would like to study ways of improving efficiency in the use of labor and natural resources. This will involve rebuilding, restoring, and upgrading a rapidly deteriorating infrastructure as well as creating new physical structures that reflect the application of modern technology. Turkey desperately needs new airports, harbors, highways, public transportation systems, and industrial plants to facilitate its rapid economic growth. The engineering problems Turkey faces require professionals who are able to bring together ideas from technology, science, and systems and operations management.

By earning an M.S. degree in Construction Engineering and Management, I will return to Turkey equipped with the most sophisticated knowledge in my field. I hope not only to learn practical information that I can apply to the situation in Turkey, but also to acquire the theoretical basis and research skills necessary to identify structural, managerial, and economic problems and formulate strategies for solutions. My ultimate goal is to be a professional with the ability to implement my vision for the future of Turkey.

1. What did this essay tell you about the student's background?

   _____

   _____

2. Why do you think the student mentioned playing with LEGO pieces in the introduction?

   _____

   _____

3. Why is the student interested in studying engineering?

   _____

   _____

4. What experiences led him to this interest?

   _____

   _____

5. How has he prepared himself for graduate school?

_____

_____

6. What qualities do you detect about this student that will make him successful in graduate school?

_____

_____

Writing a Statement of Purpose

Practice writing a statement of purpose. Respond to the following sample question.

In the space below, please discuss your educational background, career objectives, and research interests. Be as specific as you can about the area in which you plan to study.

Prewriting

A. Choose one of the prewriting techniques that you are comfortable with. Use the space below to generate ideas.

B. Organize your prewriting.

Writing

On a separate piece of paper, write the first draft of your essay.

Revising and Editing

READY TO WRITE

A. Wait at least one day and then revise your essay using the checklist on page 75. Write or type a revised version of your essay.

B. Use the checklist on page 56 to edit your essay. Correct all the grammar, punctuation, capitalization, and spelling errors. Give your essay to your teacher and someone else to read for any final comments before you copy it over or type it.

APPLICATION FOR UNDERGRADUATE ADMISSION

PERSONAL DATA

Legal name: _____

        Last   *First*   *Middle (complete)*   *Jr., etc.*   *Sex*

Prefer to be called: _____ (nickname)   Former last name(s) if any: _____

Are you applying as a ☐ freshman or ☐ transfer student?   For the term beginning: _____

Permanent home address: _____

                                         Number and Street

_____

      City or Town   *County*   *State*   *Zip*

If different from the above, please give your mailing address for all admission correspondence:

Mailing address: _____

                              Number and Street

_____ Use until: _____

      City or Town   *State*   *Zip*   *Date*

Telephone at mailing address: _____ / _____   Permanent home telephone: _____ / _____

                 Area Code   *Number*   *Area Code*   *Number*

Birthdate: _____ Citizenship: ☐ U.S. ☐ Permanent Resident U.S. ☐ Other _____ Visa type _____

      Month   *Day*   *Year*   *Country*

Possible area(s) of academic concentration/major: _____ or undecided ☐

Special college or division if applicable: _____

Possible career or professional plans: _____ or undecided ☐

Will you be a candidate for financial aid? ☐ Yes ☐ No If yes, the appropriate form(s) was/will be filed on: _____

The following items are optional: Social Security number, if any: ☐☐☐ - ☐☐ - ☐☐☐☐

Place of birth: _____ Marital status: _____

            City   *State*   *Country*

First language, if other than English: _____ Language spoken at home: _____

How would you describe yourself? Check any that apply.

☐ American Indian, Alaskan Native (tribal affiliation _____)   ☐ Mexican–American, Mexican

☐ Native Hawaiian, Pacific Islander   ☐ African–American, Black

☐ Asian American, Asian (including Indian subcontinent) (country _____)   ☐ White, Anglo, Caucasian

☐ Hispanic, Latino (including Puerto Rican) (country _____)   ☐ Other (Specify_____)

EDUCATIONAL DATA

School you attend now _____ Date of entry _____

Address _____ ACT/CEEB code number _____

         City   *State*   *Zip Code*

Date of secondary graduation _____ Is your school public? _____ private? _____ parochial? _____

College counselor: Name: _____ Position: _____

School telelephone: _____ / _____   School FAX: _____ / _____

        Area Code   *Number*   *Area Code*   *Number*   **APP**

ACADEMIC HONORS

Briefly describe any scholastic distinctions or honors you have won, beginning with ninth grade:

_____

_____

_____

EXTRACURRICULAR, PERSONAL, AND VOLUNTEER ACTIVITIES

Please list your principal extracurricular, community, and family activities and hobbies in the order of their interest to you. Include specific events and/or major accomplishments such as musical instrument played, varsity letters earned, etc. Please (✓) in the right column those activities you hope to pursue in college.

Activity	Grade level or post-secondary (PS) 9 10 11 12 PS	Approximate time spent — Hours per week	Weeks per year	Positions held, honors won, or letters earned	Do you plan to participate in college?

WORK EXPERIENCE

List any job (including summer employment) you have held during the past three years.

Specific nature of work	Employer	Approximate dates of employment	Approximate no. of hours spent per week

In the space provided below, briefly discuss which of these activities (extracurricular and personal activities or work experience) has had the most meaning for you, and why.

_____

_____

_____

_____

_____

ANSWER KEY

Chapter 1

Chapter Highlights, p. 20

1. subject, purpose, audience
2. prewriting, writing, revising, and editing
3. brainstorming, clustering, freewriting, keeping a journal
4. making a simple outline

Chapter 2

Chapter Highlights, p. 41

1. a single topic
2. topic sentence
3. controls
4. support the topic sentence
5. providing specific reasons, details, or examples
6. topic
7. focus
8. specific details
9. single focus
10. logical order
11. relate
12. time order
13. spatial order
14. order of importance
15. transitions (signals)

Chapter 3

You Be the Editor, p. 58

There are a lot of interesting things to see and do in new york city [N Y C]. It is home to over 150 world-class museums. ~~Their~~ There are art museums, science museums, photography museums, natural history museums, and even a museum of seaport history. New York is known for ~~their~~ its rich variety of theater, music, and dance. From the bright lights of Broadway and the respected stages at Lincoln Center and Carnegie Hall to the high kicks of the Rockettes at Radio City Music Hall and incredible jazz at intimate clubs, there is something for everyone. Many people go to New York, ~~For~~ for the wonderful restaurants. There are thousands of restaurants to please every palate and wallet. If you are looking for a place to shop, ~~You~~ you will find everything you can imagine. With more than 10,000 shops filled with brand names and bargains from around the world, NYC ~~are~~ is a shopper's paradise. ~~as~~ As for me, people-watching is my favorite New York pastime.

Chapter Highlights, p. 59

1. revising
2. editing
3. improve
4. add new ideas
5. eliminate irrelevant sentences
6. rearrange ideas
7. topic sentence
8. relate
9. delete
10. logical order
11. transitions
12. details
13. facts
14. examples
15. reasons
16. grammar
17. punctuation
18. spelling

Chapter 4

Chapter Highlights, p. 77

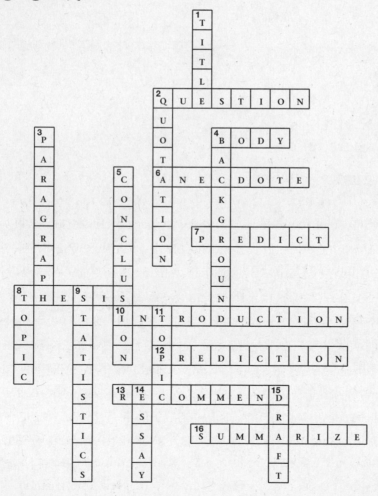

Recipe

If you like to eat or bake delicious cookies, you will love this recipe. Soften ½ pound of butter and mix it together with 2 cups of ~~a~~ sugar. Stir in 3 beaten egg[s] and 3 tablespoons of lemon juice. Then add 4 cups of flour, 1 teaspoon of baking powder, and 2½ teaspoons of nutmeg. As soon as the mixture is thoroughly combined, form the dough into a large ball and refrigerat[e] it for at least 1 hour. When ~~your~~ [you're] ready to bake the cookies, divide the ball of dough in half. Roll the dough out so that [it] is ⅛ inch thick. It will be easier if you use a rolling pin. Cut the cookies into shapes, using the open end of a glass or cookie cutters if you have them. Put the cookies on greased cookie sheets and bake them at 375 degrees for 6 minutes. To make them sweeter and more festive, frost them with colored frosting. With this recipe, the hardest part is trying not to eat t[o]o many!

Chapter 6

You Be the Editor, p. 99

Consumer products are usually divided into three groups[:] convenience, shopping, and specialty products. Each group is based on the way people buy[,] products. Convenience products are products that a consumer needs but that he or she is not willing to spend very much time or effort shopping for. Convenience products [are] usually inexpensive, frequently purchased items. Some common examples are bread, newspapers[,] soda, and gasoline. Buyers spend ~~few~~ [little] time planning the purchase of a convenience product. [They also] ~~Also~~ do not compare brands or sellers. The second group, shopping products, are those products that customers feel are worth the time and effort to compare with competing products. Furniture, refrigerators, cars, and televisions are examples of shopping products. Because these products are expected to last a long time[,] ~~They~~ [they] are purchased less frequently than convenience products. The last group is specialty products.

Specialty products are consumer products that the customer really wants and makes a special effort to find and buying. Buyers actually plan the purchase of a specialty product. They know what they want and will not accept a substitute. High-tech cameras, a pair of skis, and a haircut by a certain stylist are examples of specialty products. In searching for specialty products, Buyers do not compare alternatives.

Chapter 7
You Be the Editor, p. 114

The Great Depression of the 1930s affected Americans for generations. The complete collapse of the stock market began on October 24 1929, when 13 million shares of stock were sold. On Tuesday, October 29, known as Black Tuesday, more than 16 million shares were sold. The value of most shares fell sharply, resulting in financial ruin for many people and widespread panic through the country. Although there have been other financial panics. None has had such a devastating and long-term effect as the Great Depression. By 1932, the industrial output of the United States had been cut in half. One-fourth of the labor force, about 15 million people, was out of work, and hourly wages dropped almost 50 percent. In addition, hundreds of banks will fail. Prices for agricultural products dropped to their lowest level since the Civil War. More than 90,000 businesses failed complete. Statistics, however, cannot tell the story of the extraordinary hardships the masses of americans suffered. For nearly every unemployed people, there were dependents who needed to be fed and housed. People in the United States had never known such massive poverty and hunger before. Former millionaires stood on street corners trying to selling apples at 5 cents apiece. Thousands lose their homes. Because they could not pay there mortgages. Some people moved in with relatives. Others moved to shabby sections of town and built shelters out of tin cans and cardboard. Homeless people slept outside under old newspapers. Many Americans waited in lines in every city, hoping for something to eat. Unfortunately, many of these people died of malnutrition. In 1931 alone, more than 20,000 Americans committed suicide.

Chapter 8

You Be the Editor, p. 127

Now that I am pregnant with our first child, my husband and I will have to find a bigger place to live. Our little apartment in the city is too small for three people. We ~are~ trying to decide whether we should get a bigg~er~ apartment in the city or move to the suburbs. We have four main considerations: expense, space, convenience, and schools. In general, ~it~ is probably ~~expensiver~~ more expensive to live in the city. On the other hand, we would have to buy a car if we moved to the suburbs. ~W~e would also have to buy a lawnmower and a snowblower or hire someone to care for the lawn and driveway. In terms of space, we could definitely have a bigger house and much more land if we lived in the suburbs. However, we wonder if it would be worth it, since we would lose so many conveniences. Stores would be farther away, and so would friends, neighbors, movie theaters, museums, and restaurants. The ~~most~~ biggest inconvenience would be that we would both have to commute to work every day instead of walking or taking the bus. The ~S~chools are probably better in the suburbs, but for our child, who isn't even born yet, school is several years away. In looking at our priorities, it becomes clear that we should continue to live in the city for now and then reevaluate our decision as the baby gets closer to school age.

Chapter 9

You Be the Editor, p. 139

If you are like most people, you average one to three colds per year. Even if you do not have a cold right now, the chances are three in four that within the next year, at least one cold virus will find you. Then you'll spend a week or so suffering from the miseries of the common cold: fatigue, sore throat, laryngitis, sneezing, stuffy or runny nose, and coughing. According to researchers, colds are the most common medical reason for missing school and work. Once you catch a cold, what can you do? There is no known cure yet for a cold. There are, however, several things you can do to suppress the symptoms so that you feel better while the virus runs its course. For example, make sure that you get plenty of sleep and drink lots of liquids. You may find commercially available cold remedies such as decongestants, cough suppressants, and expectorants helpful, but keep in mind that these products can cause side effects. Many people prefer home remedies such as chicken soup, garlic, and ginger tea. In treating a cold, remember the wisdom of the ages, "If you treat a cold, it will be gone in a week; if you don't treat it, it will be gone in seven days."

Source: *Jane Brody's Cold and Flu Fighter*

Chapter 10

You Be the Editor, p. 151

In the article "The Growing of Green Cars," W. E. Butterworth discusses the new trends in environmentally safe automobiles called "green cars." Automakers are working hardly to produce cars that cause less pollution. Their long-term goal is to make zero-emission vehicles (ZEV) to comply with new state laws. The author mentions several ways that car companies can reach their goal, such as designing cars that burn less fuel, tuning engines so they burn more cleaner fuels, and producing electric cars that do not burn any fuel. However, each one of these solutions has a drawback, and many of them are expensive. Although everyone agrees that there are no simple solutions, More and more states are adopting stricter antipollution laws.

Chapter 11

You Be the Editor, p. 163

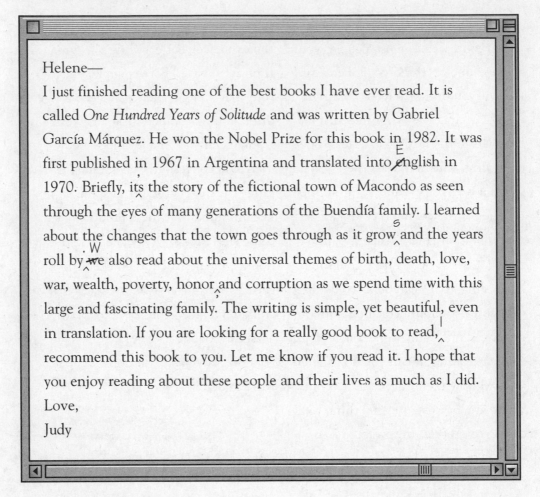

Helene—

I just finished reading one of the best books I have ever read. It is called *One Hundred Years of Solitude* and was written by Gabriel García Márquez. He won the Nobel Prize for this book in 1982. It was first published in 1967 in Argentina and translated into English in 1970. Briefly, its the story of the fictional town of Macondo as seen through the eyes of many generations of the Buendía family. I learned about the changes that the town goes through as it grows and the years roll by. We also read about the universal themes of birth, death, love, war, wealth, poverty, honor and corruption as we spend time with this large and fascinating family. The writing is simple, yet beautiful, even in translation. If you are looking for a really good book to read, I recommend this book to you. Let me know if you read it. I hope that you enjoy reading about these people and their lives as much as I did.

Love,

Judy

Chapter 12

You Be the Editor, p. 170

I am interested in mathematics and science, but at this point I have not yet identified a specific area to major in. I am also interested in learning more about the field of engineering. At Blake University I can explore all of these areas before I decide upon a major. Blake even offers the opportunity to combine them into an interdisciplinary major. Finally, although I do not intend to major in art, I have a strong interest in art and find the ~~possible~~ possibility of taking courses at Blake's School of Design attractive.

Credits

page 6. From *Dave Barry's Only Travel Guide You'll Ever Need*, by Dave Barry, Fawcett Columbine Books, New York, 1991, pp. 19, 20.

page 25. Source: *Dos and Taboos around the World*, edited by Roger Axtell, John Wiley and Sons, Inc., New York, 1993.

page 25. Source: *Encarta 1994*, "Pets." Microsoft.

page 34. Source: *Car and Travel*, "Seven Stress-Busters for Air Travelers," by Anne Kelleher, Nov.–Dec. 1995, pp. 8–9.

page 36. From Carol Varley and Lisa Miles, *The USBORNE Geography Encyclopedia*, E.D.C. Publishers, Tulsa, Oklahoma, p. 24.

page 65. From "Pet Therapy," Sy Montgomery, *Cobblestone*, June 1985, p. 21.

page 69. From "Sleeping Well," Nick Gallo, *Your Health and Fitness*, p. 7.

page 69. Source: *Conde Nast Traveler*, "How Safe Is Flying?" by Gary Stoller, Dec. 1995, pp. 116–118.

page 84. Sources: *Psychology*, 2d ed., Diane E. Papalia, Sally W. Olds, McGraw-Hill Book Co., New York, 1988, p. 175. *Cat Catalog*, edited by Judy Firemen, "How to Teach Your Cat to Shake Hands," by Ken Von Der Porten, Workman Publishing Co., Inc., New York, 1976, pp. 289–290. *Introduction to Psychology*, 11th ed., Rita Atkinson, Richard Atkinson, Edward Smith, and Daryl Bem, Harcourt Brace College Publishers, New York, 1993, p. 267.

page 106. Sources: *World Book Encyclopedia*, 1989, Volume D, #5, p. 218, "Dinosaur" by Peter Dodson. *The Evolution Book*, Sara Stern, Workman Publishing Co., Inc., New York, 1986, pp. 227–228.

page 119. Sources: "The 'Jim' Twins" by Betty Springer, *Good Housekeeping*, February 1980, pp. 123, 206, 208, 210. "Double Mystery" by Lawrence Wright, *New Yorker*, August 7, 1995, pp. 49–50.

page 134. "Energy Sources: A Dilemma for the 21st century" by Alan Bronstein. Reprinted with permission.

page 139. Source: *Jane Brody's Cold and Flu Fighter*, Jane Brody, W. W. Norton Company, New York, 1995.

page 142. "What Will Our Towns Look Like? (If We Take Care of Our Planet), *Time for Kids*, January 21, 2000. Reprinted with permission.

page 145. From "New Planet May Support Life," David L. Chandler, *Boston Globe*, Jan 18, 1996. Reprinted courtesy of *Boston Globe*.

page 146. "A Chimp Off the Old Block," Curtis Rist, *Discover* magazine, January 2002. Reprinted with permission.

page 148. "Politics As Usual" by Diana Childress. From *Cobblestone* April 1995 issue: *Franklin D. Roosevelt*, © 1995, Cobblestone Publishing, Inc., 30 Grove Street, Suite C, Peterborough, NH 03458. Reprinted by permission of Carus Publishing Company.

page 150. "Wayne Gretzky: A Hockey Hero" by Daniel Lourie. Reprinted with permission.

page 160. "The Road Not Taken" from *The Poetry of Robert Frost*, Henry Holt and Company, Inc., New York, 1916. Reprinted by permission of the publisher.

page 161. "Hope Is the Thing with Feathers" by Emily Dickinson. Reprinted courtesy of Harvard University Press.

page 167. "Taking the Plunge" by Matthew Root. Reprinted with permission.

page 170. Statement of Purpose for graduate school essay by Hasan Halkali. Reprinted with permission.